Saints for Our Time

SAINTS
for our time

Rev. David Q. Liptak

Arena Lettres • New York

NIHIL OBSTAT: Thomas J. Lynch
                  Censor Deputatus

IMPRIMATUR: ✠ John F. Whealon
                  Archbishop of Hartford

                  December 7, 1975

Printed in the United States of America

Library of Congress Catalog Card No. 76-45725

ISBN: 0-88479-002-9

To the
Queen of all Saints
And to
One of Her Sons
Albertus Magnus

Foreword

Loneliness is a mark of this age. Our shrunken world is a community of the solitary, the distance from heart to heart greater than ever before. Our crowded cities count among their chock-a-block residents all too many who are utterly friendless.

If only they knew it, they have friends in plenty. First, and incomparably, there is God, whose fatherly love embraces all. Then there are the saints, God's particular friends and benevolently disposed to all of us, their lesser fellows.

This book is a gallery of portraits in miniature of certain saints. The subjects, skillfully limned, are various as to type and station, age and place. That is, they are representative of the human family in all its shades and complexities. Each one demonstrates, in his or her own way, how one advances in the divine friendship and in that divinely commanded charity toward others which is the best and most enduring element in human friendship.

The reader will find all the saints here represented interesting and inspiring. But some one or some few will particularly appeal to him and bring him the light, the leading, the quickening of love, for time and for eternity, which he has long sought.

REV. MSGR. JOHN S. KENNEDY

Introduction

Before the 1970's, the Church's liturgical year commemorated a saint nearly every day. The Second Vatican Council, however, decided that clearer attention should be given to Jesus Christ and to our salvation through the Lord's suffering, death and resurrection.

As a result, fewer saints are found in the liturgical calendar. Those whom we meet, as each liturgical year moves on, are the Apostles and the outstanding heroes and heroines of the faith. They form a yearly procession representing the various centuries, cultures and countries of this universal Church.

So we should come to know these friends of God. In their struggles and triumphs we should find example and encouragement.

For that reason this book, *Saints for Our Time*, is warmly recommended. Its presentation of selected saints is brief, interesting and scholarly. It describes what other women and men have done for God in their lifetimes — and what we also should try to do.

MOST REVEREND JOHN F. WHEALON
Archbishop of Hartford

A Note for the Paperback Edition

The dates for the saints' feasts or memorials cited in this book conform to the new general Roman Calendar of March 21, 1969. In cases where a date is not given, Number 56 of the Roman Calendar applies. According to this directive, the celebrations of those saints' days not listed in the Calendar are assigned to the days on which these saints died. When a saint's date of death is not known, his or her memorial may be kept on a day associated for some reason with the saint; his ordination date, for example.

This paperback edition includes pieces on Elizabeth Ann Seton, the first native-born saint of the United States, Oliver Plunket, and John Nepomucene Neumann.

In an appendix, moreover, Pierre Toussaint, Bishop Frederic Baraga, and Venerable Kateri Tekakwitha have been added because of their special relevance to the United States of America.

Contents

Liturgical Index

The saints in this book are here listed according to their months and dates in the current Roman Calendar. Solemnities are designated by the letter S; Feasts, by F; Obligatory Memorials, by M; Optional Memorials, by O.

January

4 St. Elizabeth Ann Seton: M
5 John Nepomucene Neumann: M
13 St. Hilary of Poitiers: O
17 St. Anthony of Egypt: M
21 St. Agnes: M
24 St. Francis de Sales: M
28 St. Thomas Aquinas: M

February

3 St. Blaise: O
14 SS. Cyril and Methodius: M

March

8 St. John of God: O
9 St. Frances of Rome: O
17 St. Patrick: O
19 St. Joseph: S

April

4 St. Isidore of Seville: O
25 St. Mark: F

May

14 St. Matthias: F
25 St. Bede: O

June

1 St. Justin: M
3 The Martyrs of Uganda: M
5 St. Boniface: M
13 St. Anthony of Padua: M
21 St. Aloysius Gonzaga: M
24 St. John the Baptist: S
29 St. Peter: S
30 The Martyrs Under Nero: O

July

6 St. Maria Goretti: O
11 St. Benedict: M
14 St. Camillus: M
31 St. Ignatius Loyola: M

August

1 St. Alphonse de Liguori: M
4 St. Jean Vianney: M
10 St. Lawrence: F
19 St. John Eudes: O
20 St. Bernard: M
21 St. Pius X: M
27 St. Monica: M

September

27 St. Vincent de Paul: M

October

4 St. Francis of Assisi: M
9 St. Dionysius: O
16 St. Hedwig: O
18 St. Luke: F
19 St. Antoine Daniel: M
19 St. Isaac Jogues: M
19 St. Jean de Brebeuf: M
19 St. Noel Chabanel: M
19 St. Rene Goupil: M
23 St. John Capistran: O

November

3 St. Martin de Porres: O
10 St. Leo the Great: M
11 St. Martin of Tours: M
13 St. Frances Xavier Cabrini: M
15 St. Albertus Magnus: O
17 St. Elizabeth of Hungary: M
22 St. Cecilia: M
30 St. Andrew the Apostle: F

December

4 St. John Damascene: O
13 St. Lucy: M
26 St. Stephen Protomartyr: F
27 St. John the Apostle: F
28 The Holy Innocents: F

Saints for Our Time

All Saints   ✠

For tales of love and sheer adventure, nothing can surpass the lives of the saints. No heroes from the pages of fiction, nor giants of ballad or song, nor leaders and geniuses of history can, in any combination, stand up to a single cross section of these remarkable men and women of God. Theirs, by far, are the greatest stories ever written.

What novelist, for all his imaginative skill, could have created a heroine like the Maid of Orleans? What dramatist could have written a scene comparable to the one in which St. Isaac Jogues asks special permission to celebrate Mass with fingers chewed to the bone by the savage Indians of the New World? What poet could have conceived of a story of marital happiness like that of King Louis of Bavaria and his child bride, St. Elizabeth of Hungary?

A modern plot? With a modern theme? What of the ordeal of St. Maria Goretti, the little Italian girl of our very generation who was martyred for her purity? The man who murdered her testified at her canonization proceedings. Could there be a greater final chapter to a book than that? A more dramatic closing act?

Perhaps the greatest paradox about the saints is that they are not really so unlike ourselves after all. Their fundamental makeup and ours is the same; the difference is in the finished product.

Saints and sinners alike, we were all created by God to reflect His glory; principally for this we came into the world. For a metaphor, our souls are mirrors of the Divine Perfection.

Like mirrors, our souls have a tendency to become

dusty and scratched — even dirty. To retain their baptismal luster they must be polished again and again with the agent of sanctifying grace. Without grace, constantly applied, they can become so dull that God hardly sees His reflection therein.

The difference between a saint and ourselves then is the difference between a sparkling mirror and a dark mirror. The saints became saints precisely because they worked so hard upon the mirrors of their souls that God saw Himself reflected there, in all His brilliance. And that, of course, should be the work of every true child of God.

A final consideration, from the metaphor. Even a broken mirror retains its potency to reflect. Though smashed into a hundred pieces, it can still be made to return the rays of the sun. The Magdalen was one example; St. Augustine, another.

St. Albertus Magnus ✠

The awesome genius of St. Albert the Great is eclipsed by that of few other men in history, among them, of course, his peerless protégé, the Angelic Doctor of Aquin himself. So much can be inferred from the fact that St. Albert's own contemporaries dubbed him "the Great," recognizing him as "no less godlike in all knowledge," the "wonder and miracle" of their age — the same age that also produced such mental giants as St. Bonaventure, Roger Bacon, and Alexander of Hales.

Of German nobility, he attended the University of Padua before entering the Dominicans, in the face of severe parental opposition. By 1228 he was already lecturing at Cologne. Next, in succession, he taught at Hildesheim, Freiburg, Regensburg (where many years later he was to serve as bishop for a brief interim), Cologne again, then Paris. In 1248 he returned to Paris where he met St. Thomas.

His amazing knowledge, partially recorded in writings that fill 38 large volumes, embraced nearly every science known in his time. His crowning achievement, of course, was the preparatory work he did for the wedding of Christian theology to Aristotelian methods and principles; in this way, he was the proximate precursor of the Scholastic System formulated by St. Thomas.

But his successes in the higher sciences were equaled by his accomplishments in the physical sciences. Thus, he was an authority in physics, chemistry, zoology, botany, human physiology, geography, astronomy, and mineralogy. Because of his insistence upon observation, experimentation, and induction in explaining natural phenomena, he merits recognition as a pioneer in the so-called scientific method.

St. Albert was lecturing at Paris in 1278 when his memory suddenly failed. A gradual mental deterioration followed, ending with his death two years later.

As a youth, he once said that our Blessed Lady appeared to him, promising to obtain for him extraordinary intellectual graces if he would persevere, but that these graces would be withdrawn in his old age.

This story serves to underscore the key to St. Albert's sanctity. He knew, in short, that of himself he was nothing; that every talent he owned, he received from God; that the only reason for his genius was the honor and glory of God; that, used rightly his brilliance could be his own personal ladder to holiness.

Thus it is with all human beings. Intellectual brilliance is, after all, a gratuitous gift from God to a clod of clay.

Granted for God's glory, it can be used with such perfection that it can make a man a saint. Abused for man's own ambition, it can lead to eternal perdition.

St. Agnes ☩ JANUARY 21

A twelve-year-old girl dragged across the floor to a pagan altar and told to renounce her virginal chastity before a curious throng of debauchees, while the torturer waits with his irons — this is the scene which typifies the child-martyr, St. Agnes.

The details of her life are not known. Some have been hopelessly confused in the mists of legend. The clear fact is that she lived in Rome during the early persecutions, was subjected to painful and ignominious tortures in an effort to force her to desecrate her virginity, and steadfastly refused. Just before she died, according to tradition, she brushed back the hair from the nape of her neck for the axman's stroke.

The thought of a twelve-year-old girl enduring public humiliation, exquisite torture, and death rather than yield her virginal chastity may at first sound rather extraordinary to the modern world. But then we think of St. Maria Goretti in our own century. Moreover, we find another parallel right at hand when we consider the numberless young people being dragged to the pagan idols of today by the very society they live in; the moral tortures they must continually face in defense of their virtue against the sordid and indecent suggestions flaunted by billboards, magazines, newspapers, films, television programs, stage shows; the constant temptation they must withstand in the factories and offices where they work.

St. Agnes is a model for all the modern youth who struggle daily to guard their virtue. Her life presents indisputable proof that one may remain completely unstained no matter how difficult the struggle, how excruciating the torment. From heaven she helps all who seek to remain pure.

St. Alice ☩

Of his *Alice in Wonderland*, Lewis Carroll once wrote: "The why of this book cannot . . . be put into words. Those for whom a child's mind is a sealed book, and who see no divinity in a child's smile, would read such words in vain; while for anyone who has ever loved one true child, no words are needed. For he will have known the awe that falls on one in the presence of a spirit fresh from God's hands, on whom no shadow of sin, and but the outermost fringe of the shadow of sorrow, has yet fallen; he will have felt the bitter contrast between the selfishness that spoils his best deeds and the life that is but an overflowing love. . . ."*

Except for one questionable phrase in this apologia, Carroll has scored a direct hit upon the mysterious relationship between childlikeness and holiness. For a study of this relationship in a particular person, one can hardly find an example more appropriate than the medieval maiden who bore the same name as the polite little daughter of Oxford's Dean Liddell, for whom

---

* From *Alice in Wonderland*, by Lewis Carroll (New York: Modern Library Edition, Random House).

Carroll, then a lecturer at Christ Church, composed his fantasy almost a century ago: St. Alice, of course.

Simplicity and pure, disinterested love characterized the entire life of this friend of God, born near Brussels around 1200. At seven she received her parents' leave to grow up among the Cistercian nuns of a nearby cloister. Upon attaining the required age, she entered the community.

As a religious she retained every bit of her childlike innocence. In loving God, her soul was as open and free from distraction as the wide eyes of a little girl awe-stricken with the magic of creation. For her heavenly Father she actually thrilled in doing things for others. Not a shade of selfishness or hope of reward crossed her motivation; she just went about expending herself for the same pure reason a child surprises its mother by sweeping the kitchen or doing the dinner dishes.

Simple though her life was — and here is where Lewis Carroll erred in relating childlikeness to sanctity — it was not free of sorrow. Of sadness, yes, but not of sorrow, which comes in consequence of original sin. While still in the springtime of her youth she was stricken with leprosy and had to be isolated. For long years then she wasted away, until her strength, her eyesight, her painful smile were all gone. She died in great agony, on the feast of St. Barnabas, in 1250. Her cult was officially recognized by Pope Pius X, the pope of little children, in 1907.

St. Alice's secret? That the whole world is a wonderland to anyone who looks at it with the eyes of a child, to anyone who lives it like a game of hide-and-seek with the Eternal Father, who can be found everywhere. And also that suffering serves as but a polishing agent for the looking glass of one's soul, so that the Father can see Himself mirrored therein in all His glory.

St. Aloysius Gonzaga ✠

His father's attempt to dissuade St. Aloysius Gonzaga from entering the religious life is difficult to understand. Don Ferrante must have noticed the nascent sanctity in his son. He must have realized, too, the supernatural nature of a vocation, and the serious penalty for human interference in such a matter. Yet in his passion for self-glory, the Marquis of Castiglione envisioned his eldest son only as a great military leader, celebrated throughout all the courts of Europe. And he was determined to do all in his power to make his dream come true.

St. Aloysius was born in his father's castle in Lombardy, in 1568. His mother was a lady of honor to the wife of Philip II of Spain. Over her objections Aloysius was introduced to army life when he was only five, when he accompanied Don Ferrante to a military encampment. It was on this occasion (as the famous story goes) that Aloysius loaded and fired a fieldpiece in the middle of the night.

His own ideas about life began to form when he was but seven. He then started to read the Little Office of our Lady and to perform minor penances and mortifications. If Don Ferrante noticed, he did not seem to care.

Obedient to his father's orders, Aloysius traveled to Florence, to the court of the Medici, where, he was told, a young man could get ahead. But to him the grand ducal society was one "of fraud, dagger, poison, and lust . . ." and he would have no part of it.

Instead of spending his time in the revels and idle recreations of the palace, he frequented the churches of Florence, often rising at midnight to pray. He increased his penances. He took a vow of chastity. And he decided, once for all, to enter the Society of Jesus.

Don Ferrante flew into a rage when he heard of it. Hoping to change his son's mind, he forced Aloysius to appear at the courts of Mantua, Ferrara, Parma, and Turin. There were other schemes. But they were of no use. Aloysius entered the Society on November 25, 1585.

His life as a Jesuit was brief, for he died just six years later at the age of 23, as he helped the sick and dying of the great Roman plague of 1591. During his last weeks on earth he was so weak that he had to prop himself against the wall in order to kneel.

Shortly after his son became a Jesuit, Don Ferrante died, but not before he had repented and performed severe penances. As he lay dying he realized only too well the answer to a question some men still refuse to ask themselves today: "What honor is there in a parent's being able to say: 'I am largely responsible for barring my children from God's special service, to which He has called them'?"

St. Alphonse de Liguori ✠

In just eight years of practice before the bar, St. Alphonse de Liguori succeeded in achieving widespread renown as one of the most brilliant young lawyers in Naples. As a result he found himself being drawn more and more into the center of Neapolitan society.

Fortunately he was prudent enough to avoid any serious entanglement in the worldly sophistication surrounding him. From childhood he had disciplined himself in the practice of prayer and penance — in effect, he had already laid the groundwork for future sanctity. Fearful, though, that he would weaken that groundwork, he searched his soul for an escape from his newfound fame and its consequent spiritual hazards.

The solution came at court one morning. While arguing a lawsuit, he inadvertently built his case on a serious misconception of a key point. When the blunder was noted by the opposing counsel — the implication was that there had been a deliberate attempt to deceive — Alphonse was so shaken that he gave up law on the spot. Shortly afterward, he placed his sword upon the altar in the church of Our Lady of Ransom, and pledged himself to enter the ecclesiastical state.

Indefatigable is the only word capable of describing his priestly labors. From his ordination in 1726 right through to 1752, he preached missions throughout the kingdom, concentrating upon the rural regions, where knowledge about the Faith was extremely poor.

In 1731 he realized the establishment of a community of Sisters, organized largely through his efforts. And in 1732 his Congregation of the Most Holy Redeemer came into being. (The story of the early history of this great congregation of priests is a complex tale of almost incredible disappointments and problems of all kinds.)

As a spiritual writer, St. Alphonse penned countless pamphlets (the Way of the Cross commonly used in our churches during Lent is his) and about fifty books.

He is best remembered, of course, as the prince of moral theologians. In an unprecedented decree issued by the Holy See in 1831, confessors were given permission to follow St. Alphonse's opinions without weighing the reasons underlying them.

Consecrated bishop of Sant' Agata dei Goti at the age of 66, he continued to expend himself until sickness and old age set in. He died in 1774 after many physical and spiritual trials.

His secret? As a young priest, St. Alphonse made a vow never to lose a moment of time in his priesthood. He realized fully the consequences of the truths that we are all nearing eternity more closely each day, that we are going this way but once, and that we shall never be this way again.

St. Andrew Bobola ☖

"But the souls of the just are in the hand of God: and the torment of death shall not touch them." These words, from the Book of Wisdom, are especially applicable to the martyrdom of the valiant seventeenth-century Polish priest, St. Andrew Bobola.

Of noble birth, he rejected a life of wealth and luxury to enter the Jesuit novitiate at Vilnyus in 1609. (During his lifetime Poland and Lithuania were still joined together in the union forged two centuries earlier through Queen Hedwig's marriage to Duke Jagiello of Lithuania, of which Vilnyus was once the capital.)

A few years after ordination to the priesthood, Father Bobola was named superior of the Jesuit house at Bobruisk. He accepted the honor in obedience and humility, though his heart was set upon another work: that of reclaiming the scores of schismatics and lapsed Catholics in Poland and Lithuania.

As it was, he still found time to conduct some missions, for which he came to be revered far and wide. His reputation was greatly enhanced by the heroic charity he manifested toward the sick during a plague.

Father Bobola had already passed his twentieth year in the priesthood when he was finally given leave to devote himself entirely to missionary preaching. But times had changed for the worse. Eastern Orthodox factions and Protestants had joined in a campaign against Catholicism. And at the same time, hordes of Cossacks, Tartars, and Russians were making frequent raids across the Polish plains.

Driven from their churches and schools, the Jesuits took refuge in the marshes of Podlesia, eventually regrouping near Pinsk, on an estate turned over to them by a sympathetic noble.

In May, 1657, however, Cossack horsemen penetrated near the Jesuit retreat and found Father Bobola. Clubbing him brutally, they demanded he renounce the Faith. Infuriated by his adamant refusal, they roped him to their saddles and dragged him to the public slaughterhouse in Janow. Then commenced an orgy of torture. Hours later, the riders threw the seared, mutilated, partially dismembered body of the holy priest upon a refuse heap, and rode off in search of further sport.

In 1730, when the remains of Father Bobola were medically examined, his body was found to be perfectly incorrupt.

This was God's way, no doubt, of saying to his, and to all persecutors: "Dead? Only fools think so."

For, in the words of the antiphon from the Common of Martyrs, "The youth of the saints shall be renewed like the eagle's: as the lily shall they flourish in the city of God."

St. Andrew the Apostle ✠

After his brother, St. Peter, none of the original twelve Apostles was more privileged by coincidence of events than St. Andrew.

Thus he happened to be the first disciple called by our Lord. He had been with St. John the Baptist when the latter pointed to the Messias and said, "Behold the Lamb of God." On that occasion Andrew introduced himself to the Savior, accompanied Him home, and spent the remainder of the day with Him.

In the natural order of events, Andrew was also responsible for Peter's having met Christ. For after his initial conversation with the Redeemer, "the first thing he did was to find his brother Simon, to whom he said, We have found the Messias . . . and he brought him to Jesus" (Jn 1:41). It was then that Simon's name was changed to Peter — "the Rock."

With his brother, Andrew was also the first disciple accepted for Christ's permanent ministry as a "fisher of men." Significantly, his name is included second only to Peter's in the lists of the Apostles given by the first and third evangelists. (St. John gives no list, whereas St. Mark includes Andrew among the first four Apostles.)

After the Resurrection, St. Andrew probably preached in Scythia, the ancient land which corresponds to southern Russia. At least, Eusebius, the early Church chronicler, tells us this. If so, it means that Andrew had the added privilege of planting the faith in one of the greatest nations outside the Roman world of his time. (He is the patron saint of Russia.)

According to the legend, he was crucified at Patras in Achaia. There is a tradition (apparently not quite so ancient as formerly believed) that he was executed on a gibbet formed like an "X." Hence the expression, "St. Andrew's Cross."

Quite vividly, St. Andrew typifies the apostle of Christ — specifically, the priest. His privileges were incomparable — he was admitted into the Savior's inner circle! Yet his burdens, sufferings, and subsequent death, so like his Savior's, were equally incomparable, at least insofar as the world of men is concerned. Christ promised as much. For the test of an apostle is one's ready response to the Savior's question: "Can you drink the cup of which I am about to drink?"

St. Anthony of Egypt ✠

Throughout history, the truly great men — the men who have exerted the most profound influence on the ages — have been the silent men. A clear example: St. Anthony of Egypt.

He was only 18, when, in 269, he inherited his parents' rich estates bordering the Nile Delta. And, as was his right, he began to enjoy his new fortune in as Christian a manner as possible.

Six months later he chanced, while in church, to hear our divine Lord's advice to the rich young man: "If thou wilt be perfect, go, sell what thou hast, and give to the poor, and thou shalt have treasure in heaven; and come, follow me." Deeply moved, Anthony applied the words literally to himself.

Transferring his entire wealth to the poor of his village, he retired from the world under the direction of a saintly mystic, from whom he began to learn the

13

hard rudiments of the spiritual life. Then, after fifteen years of silent preparation, he plunged into the desert to seek God, alone.

There, in an abandoned fortress along the Nile, he lived in almost continuous communion with his Creator in a close mystical union. He interrupted his meditation rarely; for periodic manual labor for example, or the one meal of bread and water he allowed himself daily after sunset. Six years later he left this retreat for a lonelier one, a cliff fronting the Red Sea. His thought: to guard against the most remote possibility of any distraction whatsoever.

But distractions were inevitable, for, ironically enough, the silent man was now known throughout the world. Pilgrimages and caravans had happened upon the saintly hermit of the desert, and they brought back word of him to the cities.

Crowds flocked to listen to Anthony, to seek his advice, even to get a glimpse of him. And many men begged him to lead them on the road to perfection.

For his disciples, the saint had to leave his retreat finally, first in 305, then several times later, to establish his first monasteries. They were not true cloisters, not so well organized as those of today. But in them the first seeds of monasticism took root.

St. Anthony died in 356, at an age close to 100.

By his example and instruction, St. Anthony paved the way for monasticism, certainly one of the major factors for the spiritual good and for the culture of all civilization. Two thriving monasteries founded by him, still, 1600 years after his death, symbolize that fact.

Our world has been formed not by the glory-seekers, not by the boasting politicians, not even by the world leaders, but mostly by the silent men.

St. Anthony of Padua ✠

When asked his reason for hurrying through the canonization of St. Anthony of Padua, Pope Gregory IX simply explained that he "knew the man." Thus he implied the great Franciscan's sanctity was so evident that there could be little justification in delaying official approbation to a cult already solidly founded and flourishing even beyond Italy.

Curiously enough, though Padua boasts his tomb, St. Anthony was actually a native of Portugal. Twelfth-century Lisbon was his birthplace; his baptismal name, Ferdinand.

The Portuguese, for that matter, have always claimed him as their own. Centuries after his death he was appointed an honorary captain in their armies.

As a youth, St. Anthony joined the Augustinian Canons in his home city. He was sent later to Coimbra, where he was ordained. There, too, he first met the newly organized Franciscans. A band of them was passing through on their way to missionary Morocco. Deeply moved by their zeal, he sought and received permission to enter their order.

Wearing the brown habit now, he volunteered for Morocco. He arrived there, too, but soon became so ill that he was forced to return to Europe. Put ashore at Sicily, he was eventually received into a friary on the mainland, near Forli. His chief assignment for the next few years: washing dishes and pans in the hermitage kitchen.

His oratorical talents were discovered by accident. He was present at a local ordination, and the speaker had failed to appear. Directed to ascend the pulpit, Anthony immediately established himself as a preacher.

France heard him first. The Albigensian heresy was rampant there, and someone was needed to continue where St. Dominic had left off. In 1227, Anthony was recalled to Italy, and to Padua.

He died just four years later. Yet by that time he had already occasioned the conversion of untold hundreds.

Today his statue is found in nearly every Catholic church. He holds the Christ Child (as he did in a vision once seen by one of his hosts), and in his hands is a book, symbolic of his designation, by Pope Pius XII, as a Doctor of the Church. He is particularly loved by the poor.

Just how St. Anthony ever came to be the patron for lost articles and small requests is not known for certain. Many writers, including St. Francis de Sales, assure us of his patronage in such affairs. And so do events of our own experience.

St. Antoine Daniel 🕆

Humanly speaking, one of the most successful of the Jesuit missionaries to the North American Indians in the seventeenth century was Father Antoine Daniel, a native of France who had studied law before entering the seminary. He was canonized in 1930 as one of the eight North American Martyrs.

Uniquely enough, Father Daniel's success was due in large measure to his way with children. By gaining their confidence, he was able to reach their parents — if not directly, at least by means of the Gospel stories the boys and girls would bring home.

Thus, he used to begin his work among a particular tribe by teaching the youngsters to sing simple tunes, then to chant the *Pater*, *Ave*, and the Ten Commandments, all of which he had translated into Huron rhymes. He even trained a choir for Mass and Benediction — a remarkable feat, considering the notorious ill-temper and stubbornness of Indian children.

In view of his accomplishments, Father Daniel was chosen to establish, at Quebec, what was to be the first school for Huron boys. This was one youth project at which he almost failed completely, however. The candidates (eventually there were seven of them) could not adjust to the discipline and confinement of school life. One ran away; another stole a canoe and disappeared up the river; a third had to be expelled. And to make matters worse, two of the most promising students suddenly died of disease.

Fortunately, however, the school experiment did result in great good. One of the students, Armand Andewarahan by name, proved himself so faithful a Christian that he not only brought new prestige to the Church among his tribe, but also influenced many conversions.

Returning to Huronia in 1639, Daniel began to realize phenomenal gains for the Faith. But then the dread Iroquois went on the warpath.

Daniel's village was invaded on a quiet summer morning in 1648, shortly after Mass was over. The Huron braves were no match for the savage Iroquois, who slaughtered almost all in sight, including the women and children. In the little time left, Father Daniel baptized the catechumens and reminded the others that they would all meet again in heaven. A shower of arrows pierced his body; a musket shot threw him to the ground. Then the Iroquois tore into his body and hurled it into his flaming chapel.

With such heroism the missionary of the Indian children demonstrated how really he was spiritual father to all the Hurons. For the fires that consumed his body could not have been more ardent than the fires of love for the Indians which burned in his heart. A true spiritual father to mankind, he saw all men as children of the Eternal Father, who reigns in the land of eternal youth.

St. Bede

One of the questions students of English literature or history are sometimes asked on their final examinations concerns a person known as the Venerable Bede. In terms and phrases memorized from their textbooks, they will probably identify him as the earliest chronicler of British beginnings and one of the first actual literary giants of the English language. Few, we think, will remember (or ever knew) that he is also revered as a saint of the Catholic Church.

The village in which St. Bede the Venerable was born in 673 is almost buried today beneath the northern industrial centers of Newcastle and Sunderland. Twin monasteries once stood there, dedicated to SS. Peter and Paul and built by Abbot Benedict Biscop, one of the truly intellectual lights of his day.

Entrusted to the abbot by his parents when he was only seven, Bede was raised and educated within the cloister walls. He began to love the closeness to God he experienced there. There too he developed a lasting taste for study, thinking, and writing.

So he resolved to make the monastery his home forever. He became a monk, and, at the age of thirty, was ordained to the priesthood.

Though he never left the abbeys at Jarrow and Monkwearmouth, St. Bede soon achieved renown as the leading scholar in England. What he learned he put into writing for the sake of others. He produced more than forty volumes ranging in subject matter from detailed commentaries on Sacred Scripture to technical treatises on chronology. He distinguished himself as a rhetorician and a poet. His *Ecclesiastical History of the English People* is the most complete authentic document of early English times.

For all his scholarly success, however, Bede was always the monk. Fame and renown could never alienate him from the cloister where, by his own admission, he delighted in studying, teaching, and writing in the midst of the monastery discipline and liturgy.

Nor did he ever forget that his talents were from God, not from himself. He makes this clear in the epilogue of his English history when he says:

"I, Bede, *servant of Christ* and a priest of the Abbey of SS. Peter and Paul . . . have compiled this history *with the help of God. . . .*"

To an egocentric world such as ours, these words make little sense. But intellectual prowess and the ability to write well are talents loaned to us by God. Used for the divine honor and glory, they become the means of sanctification. Used for self-glory, they lead, perhaps more quickly than anything else, to spiritual ruin.

The greater the talent, the worse the deviation in its misuse.

St. Benedict ☨

The mention of St. Benedict calls to mind the Abbey of Monte Cassino. Most people will remember that monastery from the news stories during the closing days of World War II. It was leveled by Allied bombing and mortar fire. Few will recall its real importance, however, or much about the saint who built it.

St. Benedict was born of nobility near Spoleto in 480, just four years after the Vandal invaders brought down the Roman Empire. According to tradition, he was the twin of St. Scholastica. While pursuing his education at Rome, he came face to face with an immoral society. Disgusted, he left school and the Eternal City.

Determined on nothing less than spiritual perfection, he retired at last to an almost inaccessible cave near Subiaco, where he could pray and do penance in solitude. For spiritual direction he chose a monk who lived in a nearby monastery.

Soon his holiness became known abroad, and hundreds began to seek his prayers and counsel. When a group of monks begged him to become their superior, the saint left his hermitage for his first taste of monastic life. Within a few years, which, incidentally, were filled with trial and heartache, the new abbot was ruling over a dozen model monasteries.

Around 529, he set out for Monte Cassino, a pagan district about 75 miles from Rome. Overturning idols and firing the groves, he built the great monastery that was to survive the ages as the symbol of monasticism.

Here St. Benedict wrote his famous Rule. Founded on silence, work, and prayer, it was to become a model for all monastic life in the future.

He died in 543, a few weeks after the death of his sister, and was buried with her.

Stability is the characteristic note of Benedictine life — the monk commits himself to one place, and there, in detachment from all else, gives himself to sanctification under the Rule and through the liturgy. Monte Cassino, rising anew on the same spot after every assault on it, typifies this simple steadfastness, which each of us, in his own situation, can imitate.

St. Bernard

One of the most complete geniuses and compelling personalities of all time was the great Doctor of the Church, St. Bernard of Clairvaux. His feast arrives within the octave of the Assumption of our Lady, whom he served so faithfully throughout his days. In her honor he wrote the *Missus Est*, a series of immortal homilies on the Incarnation.

Born in 1090 of brilliant French nobility, he would have followed his brothers into knighthood, were it not for the untimely death of his mother whom he loved dearly. The sudden loss struck reality into his youthful soul and occasioned his decision to embrace the monastic life.

The almost incredible details of his entrance into religion in 1113 have no parallel in history. Leading 30 of the most illustrious noblemen of his time, including four of his brothers, he knocked at the gates of the austere Cistercian abbey at Chatillon-sur-Rheine and begged admission to the cloister. Less than a year later he moved with them to a new monastery in the picturesque valley of Clairvaux where he inaugurated a monastic Rule reaching to the summit of the Benedictine ideal. Before long he had founded over 160 daughter houses throughout the continent.

The holiness and the learning St. Bernard acquired living as a poor and obedient recluse for Christ in the silence of the cloister were soon sought out by all of Europe. Kings traveled from afar to seek his counsel; scholars, scientists, and theologians, to discuss pressing problems. At the bidding of the Holy See he left the abbey many times to preach, dispute with heretics, address synods, even to announce a crusade. He was even called upon to help check a nascent schism on the part of an antipope. Everywhere the abbot was known and sought as an orator, polemicist, diplomat, reformer, and, most of all, as a saint.

He died within the stillness of Clairvaux at the age of 63. Before burial his body was placed before the statue of our Lady.

It seems strange that a monk should have exerted so great an influence on his century. But it gives us cause to think, especially in view of the confused spirituality and intellectual chaos of our own times. Would not the modern world profit the more through leaders who retreat to the cloisters of their own hearts before forcing their decisions on men? Would not we ourselves serve our fellowmen better if we had something real and concrete to give them?

As the abbot himself summed it up: "We give only from our surplus. If you would be wise, make yourself a reservoir before becoming a channel."

St. Bertilla Boscardin ✠

During the constant shellings and aerial bombardments — when the other hospital Sisters were paralyzed from fright — Sister Bertilla used to move among the wounded soldiers, easing their suffering, calming their minds. In one hand she usually fingered a rosary; with the other, she would pour hot coffee or dispense medicines for the shivering, blood-soaked men. Her angelic mercy the survivors of the Italian campaign near Treviso never forgot. Long after World War I was over, they were instrumental in raising a monument to her memory. And in 1952 scores of them were on hand in St. Peter's Basilica to witness Pope Pius XII declare her Blessed, and set October 20 as the annual date for her liturgical commemoration.

Annetta Boscardin was born of impoverished peasant stock. Her childhood was lonely and filled with sadness — there were family problems, some of which were recalled during her beatification proceedings.

Seemingly talentless and mentally slow, Annetta was ridiculed when she first disclosed her desire to enter religious life. People still smiled when she was finally accepted by the Sisters of St. Dorothy and given Bertilla as her name in religion.

Her initial year in the convent was spent in the laundry and the kitchens. Then she was sent to the municipal hospital at Treviso, presumably to learn nursing. But she was put to scrubbing floors instead.

In 1907 Sister Bertilla realized a dream: she was assigned to administer the children's diphtheria ward. To any prudent observer, she was born for this role.

When the great war broke out, Treviso soon became

a battlefield; the hospital, a front-line medical post. And Sister Bertilla was a nurse more than equal to the new station.

Later, at the express request of the military, Sister Bertilla was reassigned to a major field hospital near Viggiu. But once again she was relieved of nursing and sent back to scrubbing floors. It was only after the Armistice that she was reassigned to her beloved hospital work, through the direct intervention of the Mother superior.

This servant of the sick died of a long hard illness in 1922. Almost immediately miracles were reported at her grave.

From a human point of view, Sister Bertilla could have done much for souls had she been permitted to remain at nursing. But because she obeyed under the circumstances she achieved even more — God's special friendship by which she makes intercession for us.

St. Blaise ☖

The blessing of throats in honor of St. Blaise is, among American Catholics especially, one of the most popular benedictions in the ritual. The ceremony usually takes place in church on the saint's feastday. Two candles, fixed together so as to form a St. Andrew's Cross, are held by the priest against the throat of each individual kneeling at the altar rail, while the following words are said: "Through the intercession of St. Blaise, Bishop and Martyr, may God deliver you from ailments of the throat, and from every other evil; in the name of the

Father, and of the Son, and of the Holy Spirit. Amen."

This blessing has its origins, it seems, in the legend that St. Blaise once miraculously saved a small boy from choking to death on a fishbone. Apparently the child was brought to the saint by his mother, who knew St. Blaise as a former physician of renown. One form of the legend gives the site of the miracle as a prison of the Great Persecutions.

What is known of this saint historically could be summarized in a few sentences. Bishop of Sebaste in Armenia during the persecutions of Licinius (a colleague of Constantine who ruled the Eastern Empire in the beginning of the fourth century), he was martyred for the Faith around 316 by order of Agricolaus, prefect of Lesser Armenia and Cappadocia.

The Roman Martyrology describes St. Blaise's passio as particularly cruel. Scourged brutally, he was immured in darkness (the candles used for the blessing of throats were said to be reminiscent of a few candles secretly brought to his cell by a holy woman), then torn on the rack and beheaded.

The common motive, in seeking St. Blaise's blessing, is to seek his protection against physical throat disorders.

Yet why not ask him for protection against spiritual diseases of the throat? Why not ask him to petition extra graces for us whenever we are in danger of sinning with our voices, committing sins of irreverence, for example, or uncharity, or scandal?

Serious physical afflictions of the throat are frightening, indeed, but they cannot compare in horror with moral evils perpetrated by the abuse of our speech. After all, is it not a fact that the former would never have entered this world had the latter never occurred? Does not the mystery of suffering enter in here somehow?

St. Boniface ✠

That story about St. Boniface, the Apostle of Germany, felling the sacred Oak of Thor and building a church from its wood, is a true one and interesting. But it is unfortunate that, on the part of many persons, knowledge of the great missionary is limited to this single event, especially since he was one of the most brilliant and talented natives of England who ever lived.

He was born at Crediton around 680, of a hardy, enterprising Saxon clan that had immigrated there just a few decades earlier. His baptismal name was Winfred.

At the age of seven he entered the abbey at Exeter, where he studied under the Benedictines. Later he was transferred to Nursling. Appointed headmaster of the monastic school there, he gained a reputation as a scholar and administrator.

Shortly after his ordination to the priesthood, he was chosen to represent the Western Synod in a delicate diplomatic mission to Canterbury. So successful was he that his fame spread throughout England.

But a missionary career was now brewing in his mind. His great dream, as he himself expressed it, was of converting the territory of Saxony and Frisia, "the land of our fathers . . . whose inhabitants are of our own blood."

He sailed to Frisia, but had to return because of local wars.

Then, with new plans, he traveled to Rome. Pope Gregory II received him, gave him full authority as the personal missionary of Peter to the German peoples, and changed his name to Boniface ("he who does good").

Beginning in Bavaria, he now launched the main work of his life: the formation and organization of a

Catholic Germany. He fearlessly forged ahead, planting the Faith, establishing dioceses, building churches, schools, convents, forging Catholicism.

"Roman Germany" converted, his heart turned again to Frisia. Leaving Mainz in June of 775, he sailed down the Rhine. Shortly afterward he was martyred. He was 75 at the time.

The true greatness of St. Boniface is reflected, we think, in his last missionary journey. Here we see an old man, tired and weak, facing new worlds and dangers in his zeal for souls. He had already given his intelligence, talents, and all his days to Christ. But one thing remained: his blood. At 75 he set out to sacrifice that too, fearing only that the martyr's crown might not be his.

This is love for souls beyond human compare.

St. Camillus ☩

The first person to wear the red cross as an emblem of organized charity, St. Camillus of Lellis was already middle-aged and confirmed in a gambler's life when he realized his own soul was at stake, and the odds were against him. It was then that he began to atone for the countless injustices he had perpetrated across Europe, by dedicating himself to the sick and dying in the slums of Rome.

St. Camillus was born in the Kingdom of Naples, in 1550, of a name that might have been noble were it not for his father, a soldier of fortune, notorious for his gambling. After his mother's early death, he joined his father and acquired his vices. But his father died suddenly too, and the youth was left alone. In his sorrow he almost entered a monastery.

A leg wound he had sustained in battle now drove him to Rome, to the noted St. James Hospital, where he sought medical aid. In return for treatment he worked as an orderly, but was soon dismissed for his gambling.

Hiring himself out again as a mercenary, he gambled recklessly from camp to camp. He was not quite so wild as he had been, however, because he kept remembering St. James Hospital and the sickness and misery he had witnessed there.

When he was finally mustered out of service he was penniless. He begged at first, but was ashamed. Then he took a job as mule driver for a group of Capuchin monks.

He liked his new work, especially its surroundings. In the shadow of the cloisters he began to pray and to think so deeply that it took only a chance remark from a passing friar to set him on the road to sanctity.

Returning to St. James, he made himself a slave to the destitute sick. Encouraged by St. Philip Neri, he started his own community, rented a house for a hospital, and began to study for the priesthood.

Wearing a large red cross on his cassock, he searched the dark plague-ridden streets near the Tiber for broken and diseased bodies. Day and night he worked, hardly taking any rest, until his own labors broke him too. He died, begging God's mercy, on July 14, 1614.

St. Camillus is a patron of Catholic nursing because he saw Christ in every person for whom he cared. Not pity alone, nor a sense of sorrow over the misery of others, motivated him in his dedicated task. Both his sanctity and his success proceeded from his love of men through his love for God. Besides, one cannot become holy just by feeling sorry for people; one must love them in Christian charity.

St. Catherine Labouré ✠

The "miraculous medal" is not so called because of the miracles associated with its pious use, but because of the visions from which it originated. For the very design of the medal, down to the familiar cross, the capital "M," and the two hearts on its reverse side, was suggested by our Blessed Mother in a series of apparitions to a French sister, St. Catherine Labouré.

She was not a very significant nun, even in her own community. Quiet, almost uninteresting, she was described by her superiors as "matter of fact and unexcitable." Long after the authenticity of her visions had been established, she still refused to discuss them with anyone but her confessor and counselor, Father Aladel.

Of a poor farming family, she was the only one of many brothers and sisters not to attend school. After the death of her mother she was needed to care for the home. It was not until she was 24 that she finally realized her childhood ambition to enter the convent.

Following her postulancy with the Sisters of Charity of St. Vincent de Paul at Chatillon-sur-Seine, she was assigned to the novitiate in Paris. There her visions began.

On November 27, 1830, the principal apparition occurred. From our Lady's hands streamed forth the words, "O Mary conceived free from sin, pray for us who turn to thee." St. Catherine heard a voice directing that a medal be struck corresponding to the vision. To those who would wear it with devotion, special graces were promised.

After a thorough investigation into the facts of the

apparitions, told only to her counselor, ecclesiastical approbation for the medal was given by the archbishop of Paris. Almost overnight, the miraculous medal devotion became worldwide.

Its popularity soared as a result of the conversion of Alphonse Ratisbonne, a celebrated Alsatian Jew who halfheartedly agreed to wear it. Shortly afterward he was favored with a vision of our Lady as she appeared on the medal. In thanksgiving, Ratisbonne entered the Church and founded a new religious congregation.

St. Catherine Labouré, meantime, passed her remaining days in the convent, to all appearances unchanged by the unique privileges that had been hers. The sick and aged she nursed as a Sister of Charity could only guess at the secrets locked within her heart. Many, doubtless, did not know that she had been miraculously visited by the Mother of God.

Her life reminds us that not all the saints were living dynamos of personality and power. Some, like her, were most ordinary, undistinguished persons; uninteresting, even, to humans, but specially chosen by God. So it is with all souls.

St. Cecilia ✠

"I have a secret, Valerian, which I wish to confide to you: I am betrothed to an angel who guards my person with great zealousness. . . ." Thus echoes one of the most beautiful stories of Christian antiquity, the legend of St. Cecilia.

Legend, rather than history, because the "acts" of her life fail to meet every last requisite of the strict historical method. Indeed, some minor indications point to the slim possibility that the cult of St. Cecilia may not have originated around a virgin martyr, but rather with reference to the foundress of a church subsequently named for her. Even Rome's famed sixteenth-century statue of St. Cecilia has been the object of much controversy. According to the inscription it was modeled after her incorrupt body. Yet, as the authors of the modern version of Butler's *Lives* observe, certain experts "are not satisfied that there is any justification for the common belief that the body of the saint was found entire in 1599 just as [the artist] has sculptured it."

Despite such problems, however, two highly significant facts solidly support the legend of St. Cecilia as we know it. One is that it is unquestionably most ancient, dating from at least the fifth century. The other is that its substance figures in both the Divine Office and the Mass itself — predominantly so.

In brief, the "acts" read in this wise: Of patrician lineage, Cecilia was raised a Christian from infancy. Secretly having vowed perpetual virginity, she declined the prospect of marriage to the noble Valerian, but was compelled to accept upon her father's insistence. It was after the wedding feast that Cecilia informed her spouse about her angel.

Though a pagan, Valerian promised to respect her wishes provided she give him some confirming signs. At her bidding, then, he sought out Pope Urban, and was subsequently baptized. Later, with his brother, whom he had converted, Valerian shed his blood for the Faith. Eventually Cecilia herself was sentenced to die by suffocation in the baths of her palace. But when the prescribed form of execution failed, she was brutally beheaded.

It is easy to misread the meaning of Ct. Cecilia's

martyrdom. It is true that God gave her an angel to guard her virginity, but only because He had called her to that state, and she had freely consented for love of Him.

It is illogical to infer from her legend that persons called to the married state are not specially guarded by God.

Married couples have their angels too.

SS. Cyril and Methodius ☒

To a missioner forging new frontiers for the faith in lonely outposts abroad, one of the greatest consolations from a human point of view, is the moral support he receives from Christians everywhere, especially from those he left behind. Without the realization that his fellow Catholics believe in him and his work, his loneliness is so magnified that the mental pain he suffers may outweigh his physical hardship. Such pain must have been experienced by SS. Cyril and Methodius, the great Apostles to the Slavic nations.

SS. Cyril and Methodius were brothers born around 825, in the Greek city of Thessalonica. They served in high governmental posts before they gave up political fame for the monastic life.

They volunteered for the missions, and were sent to work among the Khazars, a Russian-like race which once inhabited the Caspian shores. Then they were chosen to Christianize the Slavs.

Keenly aware of the peculiar circumstances of their new assignment, they carefully studied the Slavic tongue. Cyril invented (or at least developed) an alphabet, and together with his brother translated part of the Bible and much of the Sacred Liturgy into Old Slavonic. Thus prepared, they left for Moravia in 869.

Though eminently successful, they drew violent criticism from the Germans, who suspected their orthodoxy. Rumors spread, and the saints were recalled to Rome to defend their cause. Pope Adrian II was so impressed with their arguments, however, that he sanctioned their methods. St. Cyril became ill while in Rome, and died there in 869.

Alone now, St. Methodius returned to Moravia, but the Germans renewed their efforts to disgrace him. In 870 he was summoned to Ratisbon by the German princes to explain his methods. There he was "denounced" and detained.

Released by order of Pope John VIII two years later, St. Methodius preached in Bohemia. Again he was checked, this time by forged letters, and made to clear himself before the Supreme Pontiff.

Aging and in poor health, he devoted the rest of his days to his Slavonic translations of Scripture and Canon Law. When he died, in April, 885, his enemies were still at his heels charging him with unorthodoxy.

SS. Cyril and Methodius are models for men of principle. Though plagued by suspicion, intrigue, and treachery, they kept going ahead, almost alone, because they knew they were right. History would vindicate them, they expected, as history has vindicated, and will always vindicate, men of principle.

St. Dionysius ☦

One of St. Paul's most illustrious converts was an Athenian intellectual, St. Dionysius the Areopagite.

Eusebius relates that he became the first bishop of Athens. According to another early chronicler, he died a martyr under Domitian. But nothing is known with absolute certainty about his life except the simple fact of his conversion and the circumstances which led to it. The rest is really not important, for it is precisely in the story of his conversion that we find matter for meditation.

The Areopagus (so-called because it stood on the hill of Ares, or Mars) was the supreme juridical tribunal in Athens. Its members included many of the greatest thinkers in the city-state, still the world's cultural capital, despite its awful humiliation by Sulla's legions in 86 B.C.

St. Paul arrived in Athens during his second missionary journey. He had decided to meet Silas and Timothy there — originally he had no intention of preaching there for any length of time on this trip. But as he approached the city on the road from Piraeus he was alarmed by the myriad pagan shrines along the way. What especially angered him was that the Greeks, who prided themselves on their intellectual prowess, could be so ignorant about the one true God, whose existence was so easily demonstrable philosophically.

Maneuvering for an opportunity to address the Areopagus on this matter, he began to stir up argumentation in the market of Agora. Soon his hoped-for invitation was forthcoming.

"Men of Athens . . ." the Apostle began his famed "sermon on the unknown god" (Acts 17:22–23). Purposely quoting from the Greek poets, he argued point for point to the existence of one personal God, a pure Spirit, the Creator of the universe, in whose hands all things are sustained. Among the fascinated listeners was Dionysius.

Sensing success, St. Paul launched into the doctrine of the Incarnation. But here he was rudely cut short. The Areopagites would listen to a philosophical treatise on God's nature and providence. But they would not even tolerate the notion of an incarnate God who was crucified for man's redemption.

Amid ridicule, Paul sadly walked away. In all his preaching he had never suffered worse defeat. Less civilized peoples given to base sins were quicker to accept the Gospel than these Athenians, reputedly trained in logic and epistemology.

After St. Paul, only a handful followed. One was Dionysius, willing and ready to swallow his pride. He became a saint.

The lesson? Obviously that intellectual pride is objectively a more formidable barrier to God's graces than is pagan licentiousness. But once a man removes that barrier, God plants the seeds, not only of conversion, but of sanctity. For such removal is accomplished only with the great pain experienced in complete self-reversal.

St. Dismas ☨

For the story of the Good Thief, we are indebted to St. Luke, often called the Evangelist of Mercy because of his accounts of the Good Shepherd and the Prodigal Son.

Two criminals — the gospel writer names neither of them — were crucified with the Savior, "one on his right hand, and the other on his left." One of them fell to blaspheming our Lord: "If thou art the Christ, save thyself and us!"

But the other, to whom Christian legend has assigned the name Dismas, rebuked the first, saying, "Dost thou not even fear God, seeing that thou art under the same sentence? And we indeed justly, for we are receiving what our deeds deserved; but this man has done nothing wrong. And he said to Jesus, 'Lord, remember me when thou comest into thy kingdom.'"

With this simple prayer, uttered from the depths of his heart, the Good Thief bore away the greatest treasure conceivable. For Christ, ever unable to cast aside a sincere act of love, turned and rewarded Dismas on the spot in a sentence so incredible one must reread it several times to believe: "Amen I say to thee, this day thou shalt be with me in paradise."

The force of the Good Thief's remonstrance to the other is contained in the question, "Dost thou not even fear God . . . ?" Dismas was reminding his companion, in effect, that even if he had no love or reverence for God, at least he ought to have a little holy fear, since Christ, who was also suffering the torments of crucifixion, was totally innocent.

The implication is that Dismas knew of our Lord's preaching and miracles. And despite a lifetime of crime, he had enough virtue alive in his soul to admit his mistake openly and ask pardon for the past. And so it was that Christ brought a notorious criminal into heaven on the day He died for the entire race.

The whole story of the Good Thief's entrance into heaven from the summit of Golgotha is replete with mystical significance. Christ's mission was to save sinners, above all; for that He came into the world and voluntarily ascended to the cross like a lamb led to slaughter. His very name was foretold in prophecy of such a mission: "And thou shalt call his name Jesus; for he shall save his people from their sins." Often He Himself admitted to such a mission: "I have not come to save righteous people, but sinners." And so St. Paul explained to Timothy: "This statement is true and worthy of full acceptance. Christ Jesus came into the world to save sinners."

St. Elizabeth Ann Seton ☥

It was November 18, 1803, on the Ligurian Sea. *The Shepherdess*, which had departed the port of New York seven weeks earlier, was at last nearing the bustling Italian port of Leghorn (Livorno). Among the passengers was a New York merchant, travelling with his wife Elizabeth — known as Betty — and their oldest daughter Anna, eight years old. He was seriously ill, racked by tuberculosis; the ocean voyage to the warm Mediterranean shores had been a last-moment family decision; a desperate measure to help him regain his health. He had friends in Leghorn, the Filicchis, who were in the banking business.

On November 19, just when the ship was about to dock, the beginning of what was to become a 30-day nightmare suddenly began. Yellow fever had been reported in New York when *The Shepherdess* set sail, but the ship carried no bill of health, hence it must tie up at the nearby "Lazaretto", or hospital, for quarantine: no one would be permitted to disembark for a month.

The Lazaretto was like a prison. Betty helped her husband and their daughter into Room Number 6, up twenty stone steps. Inside were only bare walls and a brick floor.

The Captain sent a few warm eggs and wine. At sunset, the Filicchis sent dinner and other necessities, and the poor travelers went to the grate to see their Italian friends.

The ordeal of the next few weeks was terrible. Wind, cold, dampness, all intensified the sick husband's agony, which was accompanied by severe chills, violent coughing, weakness and depression. On December 2, for example, his wife wrote in her diary that the night had been so cold that she tried to make fire with brush but was smoked out, and on December 14 she noted that the dampness was hazardous for a person in good health — "and my poor William's sufferings oh! . . ."

Day after day Betty nursed her husband, comforting him, keeping him warm, feeding him, helping him sit up from his ship's mattress on the damp floor. They passed part of every day reading the Bible together and praying. She wrote that they prayed and cried together. Once Betty and Anna sang Advent hymns in a low voice, and found consolation, momentarily forgetting prisons, bolts and sorrow, and would have rejoiced to have been singing with St. Paul and Silas.

On November 29 William felt strong enough to read the Bible himself. At Anna's request he chose the final chapter of the Book of Revelation.

Evenings, when her husband and daughter had fallen asleep, Betty often continued in prayer on her knees with her Bible in hand. And she would dream that she was home again in Manhattan, at her beloved Trinity Episcopal Church, singing hymns to her heart's content and listening to the beautiful sermons. Throughout the ordeal she kept faith. Once she wrote that she was reading to William, shivering under the bedclothes, and that she felt that God was with them, and that He was their joy and hope.

William survived the quarantine, but died shortly afterwards in Pisa, two days after Christmas. He is buried there and his epitaph begins, "Here lies the remains of William Magee Seton, Merchant of New York."

His valiant wife, surely one of the most beautiful women who ever lived is, of course, Elizabeth Ann Bayley Seton, who later became a Catholic and a nun, and, in 1975, the first native-born United States saint. This was the same woman, the mother of five, who founded the first American religious community for women and inaugurated the first American parish school.

She was born in New York in 1774 and was related to Gotham's first families, including the Barclays, the Delanceys and the Roosevelts. Her father was the city's first health officer. Elizabeth died in 1821.

Like another Elizabeth — the young bride of Louis of Bavaria — Mrs. Seton taught the world that "riches to rags" in the worldly sense does not mean the same thing in the spiritual sense. In Christ, all is wealth.

St. Elizabeth of Hungary ☩

The finest of romantic writers would find it challenging to produce a novel of marital happiness more fascinating than the true love story of Louis of Bavaria and his child-bride, St. Elizabeth of Hungary.

Louis had known Elizabeth from his teens, ever since she came to live at his father's ancestral castle, the Wartburg (in whose towers, incidentally, Martin Luther was detained three centuries later). When, as Landgrave of Hesse, he eventually took her to wife, he fully realized that her remarkable beauty was transcended only by her profound goodness. And for that, he loved her the most of all.

Not so her in-laws at the Wartburg. Jealous of her virtue, they ridiculed her for her piety, her love for prayer and penance. They disliked her especially for giving away castle funds to the poor.

Louis did his best to silence the scorners, for he would tolerate no obstacle in her path to sanctity. And he gave Elizabeth full permission to use his money as she saw fit.

Each day she fed scores who came to her hungry. She dressed orphans in warm clothes for the winter, and bought fuel for cold homes. She built two infirmaries in which she spent hours daily, nursing the diseased, comforting the dying. Once, when her hospitals were filled, she gave up her own bed to a leper.

The intense love Elizabeth and Louis bore each other has become legendary in the lives of the saints. Their happiness was brought suddenly to a close just six years after their wedding day. A runner brought the tragic news that Louis had fallen in the crusades.

Old jealousies reared their heads; and, it appears, Elizabeth and her children were driven from the Wartburg. For a while she lived with relatives. Then, having made adequate provision for her children, she renounced the world completely, taking the habit of the Third Order of St. Francis. A small cottage became her home, and next to it she established a small hospital. Three years later she died, still in her twenties.

Three years of constant prayer, penance, and selfless sacrifice, the merits for which must have been felt in part by her husband, whose hand she, a widow now, could still feel in hers. For prayer and sacrifice for her husband is a widow's particular duty and one of her greatest glories. St. Elizabeth teaches the modern generation that it is possible for a woman to be deeply happy in her marriage and at the same time deeply holy; that it is possible for a woman to have all that the average woman dreams of: a good husband, home, family — then lose all in one fell swoop, without prejudice to the real happiness in her heart.

St. Evodius   ✠

It was at Antioch "that the disciples were first called Christians" (Acts XI:26). In point of fact, they could no longer be called Jews, for they had already been named apostles of the New Testament, which had just been sealed by the death of the Divine Testator, Jesus Christ.

The term "Christian" was coined, it is thought, some time before the year 64 by the predecessor of St. Ignatius at Antioch: St. Evodius.

Practically nothing is known with certainty about the earlier details of his life. It is fairly factual, however, that he was both ordained a priest and consecrated a bishop by one of the Apostles — probably St. Peter, when he was about to depart for Rome. A sixth-century commentator adds with conviction that the Prince of the Apostles revisited St. Evodius on his deathbed, at which time he consecrated St. Ignatius to take the latter's place in Antioch.

The primitive Christian community at Antioch had special significance, because it included the first group of pagan converts, organized as such. Before their conversion, these Gentiles had been influenced by an assembly of Helenized Jews, descendants of a devout band who had migrated to Syria during the Seleucid dynasty. After Pentecost Sunday, Paul and Barnabas visited and preached to these dispersed Jews, who were soon won over to the Gospel.

The history of St. Evodius takes us back to an era when Antioch was one of the richest and most powerful cities of the world, the capital of Oriental civilization. Elegant and highly sophisticated, it boasted of its worldly glory: its palatial homes, its marble-covered streets, its sensuous gardens, its majestic monuments.

In its pride, the city remained totally oblivious of the tiny, poor community of Christians who lived in an isolated quarter.

Today, though, Antioch is forgotten, while the once small community which began there has inherited the world.

God has no need of earthly powers in order to propagate His name.

St. Felix ✠

Bookburning was the issue which occasioned the martyrdom of the third-century African bishop, St. Felix of Thibiuca. The books for which he gave his life were collections of Sacred Scripture, the liturgy, and manuscripts of the Fathers and early ecclesiastical writers.

The bookburning was decreed by Diocletian. For his own part, he would never have started a persecution **against the Christians. But he had political commitments to meet.**

So the now infamous edict of 303 was promulgated from the imperial palace: all books held in any way sacred by Christians were to be surrendered to local authorities and burned.

For a Christian to have complied with the edict would have been tantamount to apostasy, as well as sacrilege. The faithful were well aware of this fact. Most, therefore, chose to submit to torture rather than give up a single page of Holy Writ or any other sacred manuscript for the pagan bonfires. Some few, however, did weaken when confronted with pain. As a result, many invaluable ancient Christian collections (including sections of the Vatican archives) perished in Diocletian's persecution.

In proconsular Africa, the champion of the Faith was St. Felix, bishop of a See proximate to Carthage. He was singled out by the Romans for an example. Their reasoning was logical: if the bishop surrendered Church books and documents, chances were strong that the wills of scores of African Christians could be broken without too much trouble.

So they beat him mercilessly, loaded him with chains, and cast him into a foul dungeon to consider his answer under the phantoms of thirst, hunger, and fever. In a week's time they posed the same question, and received the same answer. For weeks the cruel interrogation and the torments went on, until the Romans themselves weakened. Their tortured bishop would not break, and to cover their failure, they put him to the sword.

The life of St. Felix is really unimportant when viewed next to the principle for which he died, namely, the holiness of the Bible and of all the books wherein the truths of the Faith are contained. A principle which we all know and recognize, yet one which only a persecution can help us really appreciate. A principle which the faithful of the Iron Curtain countries doubtless appreciate as well as did St. Felix, for they also have seen — and still see — the devil's bookburnings.

St. Fiacre ☨

"Fiacre," the French word for a small taxicab, derives from the fact that the first firm to hire out coaches in seventeenth-century Paris was located near Hotel St. Fiacre. The hotel is named after a seventh-century Irish-born hermit, whose feast is traditionally observed in Ireland and parts of France on September 1.

Here in America, St. Fiacre is best known as the patron of gardeners, especially the "do-it-yourself" variety. A small shrine in honor of the saint is fast becoming a necessary complement to backyard flower and vegetable plots.

The association rests partly upon history, partly upon legend. St. Fiacre is supposed to have embarked for the continent in quest of a place of solitude. Having arrived at Meaux, he was offered as much acreage as he could plow in a single day. Miraculously, the chronicles say, he was able to win for himself an enormous clearing in a secluded forest.

There he built a cell, enclosed by a garden, a chapel dedicated to the Blessed Virgin Mary, and an inn for travelers. This site eventually became the storied village of St. Fiacre.

The village evolved from a simple pilgrimage. News of St. Fiacre's extraordinary personal holiness and charity toward those in need drew thousands to the place. And when miracles were wrought through him, the crowds multiplied many times over.

Cures were still reported long after the saint's death in or around 670. Queen Anne of Austria, for example, attributed the recovery of Louis XIII to St. Fiacre's intercession. And when Louis XIV lay dangerously ill, the celebrated Bossuet initiated a novena in the saint's honor.

Selecting one specific lesson from the life of a saint so obscure, yet so popular, presents a problem. One point nonetheless immediately comes to mind insofar as St. Fiacre is known and venerated in our own country.

It is that even simple hobbies, such as backyard gardening, have their special saints. Like every licit recreation, amateur horticulture can constitute a prayer for God's honor and glory.

A small statue of St. Fiacre looking over one's miniature acre can serve as a vivid reminder of this point.

St. Frances Xavier Cabrini ☧

On Twentieth Street, just off Second Avenue, amid the tenements of Manhattan's lower East Side, stands Columbus Hospital. Not so large or imposing as the great medical centers nearby, it is an historic American landmark. For it represents the first and perhaps best known of the more than 50 charitable institutions established by the first United States citizen raised to the honors of the altar: St. Frances Xavier Cabrini.

Her cultural traditions were rooted in northern Italy, where she was born, a thirteenth child, in 1850. She would have entered some missionary sisterhood had there been one — China was the country of her predilection. As it turned out, even the local convents refused her on the grounds of poor health. For a while she tried her hand at managing a small orphanage.

Suddenly, one day, her entire future was determined. Called before the bishop of Lodi, who had heard of her zeal, she was told: "You want to be a missionary Sister.

Now is the time. I don't know of any institution of missionary Sisters, so found one yourself."

With seven disciples she took over an abandoned monastery to house her new Missionary Sisters of the Sacred Heart. The community grew rapidly in fame and numbers. Soon Pope Leo XIII himself heard about the remarkable Mother Cabrini.

It was he who finally convinced her to give up the prospect of China and to go to America instead. There the immigrants, penniless, confused, and unable to speak the language, had become the prey of unprincipled politicians and criminals.

At the invitation of New York's Archbishop Corrigan she began her missionary work by begging from door to door. Gradually benefactors came forward. Schools, orphanages, homes, and hospitals began to rise under her direction, not only in New York, but in cities all over the nation: Newark, Scranton, New Orleans, Chicago, Denver, Los Angeles, Seattle (where she took the oath of allegiance in 1909).

In December, 1917, her heart finally gave out. Cardinal Mundelein, who sang the funeral Mass, presided, just ten years later, at her beatification. And in 1947 the bells of Rome's 400 churches signaled to the world America's first citizen-saint.

The choice of Mother Cabrini as our first saint was appropriate, not only because she was so typical an American in her ways, but especially because she was an immigrant. For from immigrants and from immigrant stock this democracy was born and brought to greatness.

St. Frances of Rome ☩

"It is most laudable in a married woman to be devout, but she must never forget that she is a housewife. And sometimes she must leave God at the altar to find Him in her housekeeping." The speaker was St. Frances of Rome.

Had she been allowed to follow her own inclinations, she would have entered the convent at 11. Her parents objected to that. Their plans called for her early marriage into the illustrious Ponziano family.

A child bride, she resigned herself completely to God's will. She had vowed Lorenzo love and obedience; she would keep that promise as perfectly as she could.

She found a confidante and a loyal companion in her young sister-in-law Vannozza, who, like herself, had a predilection for prayer and solitude. The two wives worked together, prayed together, and, when their afternoons were free, went out together, bringing food and medicines into the Roman slums. One of their regular stops was a hospital where they helped nurse the diseased and dying. Back home every evening in time to dress and arrange for their traditional dinner parties, they gave their guests little cause for suspecting the nascent sanctity hidden behind their welcoming smiles and gracious conversation.

Following the death of Lorenzo's mother, Frances suddenly found herself head of the household. Protesting in vain, she resignedly determined to make her new position her unique road to sanctification. Her cherished hospital work, her visits to the poor, even her extra private devotions she relegated as secondary to her main responsibility of running the Ponziano household well.

That responsibility was lessened in 1408 when the armies of Ladislaus of Naples marched into Rome under the banners of the antipope. During the ensuing civil wars, Frances saw Lorenzo wounded, one of their sons taken hostage, their servants murdered, their riches seized, the mansion almost leveled. What was left of the building she turned into a hospital until the conflict was over in 1414.

The Great Schism healed and the Ponziano estates restored, Frances found time to establish a convent of oblates dedicated to the poor. Always the wife and house-keeper first, she herself did not enter her own community until after her beloved husband's death a few years later. Extraordinary prayer and penance filled her days now until her death in 1440.

A clear picture, the life of St. Frances of Rome, of what the life of every married woman should be. No care, no matter how noble, should ever be permitted to prejudice her main responsibility of being a housewife, a responsibility which can, of itself, lead the married woman to sanctity.

St. Francis of Assisi ✠

If St. Francis of Assisi is one of the world's most beloved saints, he is also one of the least understood, for the chivalrous troubadour of poverty was no carefree senti-mentalist who had nothing more to do than trek through lark-filled glens, singing songs promoting nature worship. (There are too many today who hold his representation of no greater value than so much ornamentation for a patio birdbath.) Nor was he merely a romantic humanitarian, who walked about in rags simply because he felt sorry for people.

No, the Poverello's story is senseless unless one is willing to accept the fact that he wed Lady Poverty only and precisely because he knew she would lead him to the heart of His divine Lord, who impoverished Himself by becoming Man, for love of man.

He was attracted to Poverty the first time he saw her in a fleeting vision from on high, but he lacked the courage to sacrifice what he must to have her. Melancholia paralyzed him. His comrades wondered why he avoided their nightly revelries through Assisi's streets. They asked if he were in love, and he did not deny. With a Princess, he said, "more beautiful and lovely" than they could know.

He prayed; he exchanged places with a beggar: still his Lady was too far above his station. Then, one day, swallowing every last inch of self-love, he kissed the hand of a leper. He wavered then no longer.

Before his bishop, Francis returned to his father all he had received from him; and, clad in a peasant's frock, walked away chanting the praises of God.

For two years he remained a hermit. Then, on the feast of St. Matthias, in 1209, as he listened to the Gospel, he was visited with an inspiration to preach repentance. A few months later he was already fulfilling his new calling. Crowds flocked to hear the Little Poor One, and they left converted. Some became disciples — the first Franciscans.

Lady Poverty brought him to the end of his quest in 1224, at the summit of Mt. Alverno. There, before the Crucified, he experienced a love that no living man dares dream, a love that left its marks upon his body in the sacred stigmata — "the ultimate seal," as Dante called it. He died two years later.

St. Francis' Lesson? That Poverty should not be feared, lest taking her, one have naught else. For Poverty can lead directly to Him beside whom all else is nought.

St. Francis de Sales ✝

"This servant of God conformed so well to the divine pattern that often I asked myself with amazement how a created being — given the frailty of human nature — could reach so high a degree of perfection . . . I am moved to see in him . . . the man who, of all others, has reproduced most carefully the love of the Son of God on earth."

So spoke St. Vincent de Paul at the death of his friend, the renowned bishop of Geneva: St. Francis de Sales.

The eulogy was well said, for if it is possible to epitomize the greatness of Francis de Sales, the summary would have to begin and end with the story of his tremendous love for souls in Christ.

From his ordination in 1593 he must have modeled his every conscious moment on the Good Shepherd of the Gospels.

He knew and loved his sheep, and they knew and loved the Savior through him. Constantly he moved among his people with Christlike humility, patience, mercy, charity. From the pulpit he preached of God's love in the simplest of terms, cautious, for all his learning, never to resort to erudition for erudition's sake. For those he could not reach personally or through sermons, he wrote countless letters, tracts, and books on the love of God. Even as a bishop he kept up his visitations, simple talks, and writing, and even insisted on catechizing children.

He was ready to lay down his life for his flock. Fearlessly he accepted an assignment to a hostile heretical community on the southern shores of Lake Geneva, and continued his mission there despite incredible hardships and frightening dangers, including several attacks by sworn assassins.

He went in search of strays. Thus, his highly successful work among lapsed Catholics, heretics, apostates, and abandoned sinners. "God and I will help you," he would tell them. "All I require of you is not to despair."

This last monition he never forgot to make. For as a youth, this future Bishop and saintly Doctor of the Church was so crushed with a temptation to despair that his health began to break under the strain. Without respite, he was obsessed with the satanic thought that his soul was damned for all eternity. Then, one day, he fell to his knees and prayed a heroic act of love: "Lord, if I am never to see Thee in heaven, this at least grant me, that I may never curse or blaspheme Thy holy Name. If I may not love Thee in the other world . . . then let me at least every instant of my brief existence here love Thee as much as I can." Then, turning to our Lady, he recited the *Memorare*.

Ahead for him lay only God's love and sanctity. For pure love given under severe temptation to despair of all is always returned by God a hundredfold — even to perfection.

St. Gaspar ✠

The name Jasper is about the closest equivalent in English to the Italian *Gasparo*. But "Gaspar" is also sometimes used, as in the case of St. Gaspar del Bufalo, a nineteenth-century religious founder.

A chef's son he was ordained in his native Rome, in 1808. When Napoleon took the Papal States shortly afterward, he was exiled with the other priests who refused to abjure their allegiance to the Holy See. The Rome he returned to after Bonaparte's fall was largely a spiritual wasteland, scarred by much doctrinal ignorance, neglect of the sacraments, and moral decadence.

A band of highly trained, expendable home missioners must be organized, the young priest thought, if the city and all Italy were to be totally reclaimed for Christ. To this end he laid the groundwork for what was finally to evolve into the Congregation of the Most Precious Blood.

Following Father Gaspar's leadership, his missioners went from village to village, preaching and administering the sacraments. The most depraved districts, instead of being bypassed, were visited first. Special conferences were conducted at night for men who, like Nicodemus in the gospel story, were too fearful, from human respect, of entering a church or going to confession in daylight. The missions usually ended with a public bonfire, at which external occasions of sin such as obscene books and murderous weapons were burned.

St. Gaspar had his enemies, too, among those who should have been friends. Many thought him revolutionary or overly dramatic (e.g., the bonfires). But he was stoutly defended by Pope Leo XII, to whom he once declared absolute obedience.

During the cholera epidemic of 1836 he fell gravely ill, but lingered for many weeks. The details of his attitude in his agony alone attest to his holiness.

That holiness, of course, was the key to his success. Yet it is interesting to note that he considered hard work as the most important natural factor in the work of being a Christopher. For this reason he insisted upon the founding of all kinds of works of charity for men and women of every age and circumstance. He wanted all his converts literally to fatigue themselves in special tasks for Christ. For he used to say, "If it is so sweet to tire ourselves out for God, what will it be to enjoy Him!"

St. Gemma Galgani ☩

Though she lived within our very own times, St. Gemma Galgani is rarely referred to today. True, her life was rather uneventful, as compared to the lives of most saints. But there is a deeper reason still: her life was so filled with suffering and sorrow that modern man would prefer not to remember her. It is almost as if he resents her tragic, all-too-real intrusion into his escapist world of papier-mâché delights and irresponsible flings.

For, from an earthly viewpoint alone, nothing but sadness surrounds the memory of this saint. Looked at from the outside, her life resembles one dark night extending from her birth in the Tuscan village of Camigliano in 1878 all the way to her death, after an agonizing illness, on Holy Saturday in 1903.

A dark night, first because of the abject, crushing poverty in which she was raised. Desperately poor, her family existed from day to day, hopeful only for enough food to keep them alive.

A dark night, too, because of physical torment. Racked with bad health from childhood, she suffered intensely from tuberculosis of the spine. Cured of this disease, evidently through the intercession of St. Gabriel of the Sorrows, she was then asked by God to bear the awful pain of the stigmata and the wounds of His scourging.

A dark night, finally, because of the ridicule constantly flung at her for her devotion and the mystical phenomena she frequently experienced. To conceal her privileges from the world she would have entered a convent — she had her heart set on the Passionist Sisters — but her health barred her from entrance therein.

Despite her sorrow, however, St. Gemma Galgani's soul was filled with the peace and joy that come from suffering in Christ's name. Witnesses to her many ecstasies, for example, record the extraordinary happiness she evidenced as she conversed with the saints, and prayed as if she were actually standing before God.

The reasons why God led Gemma Galgani to sainthood in sorrow are strongly hinted at in the fact that He took her back to Himself on Holy Saturday, the last day of Lent. He placed her in our midst and made her life as one continual Lent, that she might restore the balance, as it were, for other Lents now being abused or neglected by less worthy men.

In her life there is a divine warning that He is not too well pleased by the manner in which others, who sign themselves as His faithful, help expiate for their own sins, especially during the forty-day period so sacredly set aside for that purpose.

St. Gerard ☩

In his intense striving for self-sanctification, many a layman has been faced with the somewhat disturbing question: Is it possible that I could have done more for Christ and souls if I had entered the religious life?

St. Gerard of Aurillac once experienced such a doubt, which he immediately placed before his bishop. The answer he received was substantially the same one upon which so many other men seeking perfection in the world have based their lives since the first ages of Christianity. He was advised, in brief, that in view of his particular circumstances, he was achieving more for God's Kingdom as a layman in the world than he could accomplish in a monastery.

How was Gerard of Aurillac becoming a saint and winning souls for Christ as a layman in the world?

By his charity, for one thing. Heir to a giant fortune, he gave freely to all in need: the poor, the sick, the aged. He used his funds to build churches; temples to God that might never have been raised, were it not for him. He even helped build an abbey so that the divine praises might pour forth from the hearts of men dedicated to a life to which he was attracted but not called.

By his humility, secondly. A count by birth, he could easily have lorded it over those less noble in the eyes of the world. He could have felt entitled to official recognition for his philanthropies. Instead, he walked with ordinary people, lived as frugally as they, wore the simple clothes they wore.

Next, by his good example. Despite his wealth and prestige, he boasted of naught but his Faith. Every morning he was seen in his parish church for Mass and meditation. It was common knowledge that he lived a strictly disciplined spiritual life, that he prayed long hours daily. And despite his attempts to conceal the fact, it was also known that he performed severe fasts and penances.

By his patience in suffering, fourthly. In the very prime of his youth he became bedridden for several years. And during his final years his sight was taken away. Yet his only reaction was not bitterness, but the happiness of sharing in the pains of his Savior's Passion.

Last, by his resignation to God's will. Though the world seemed foreign to him; though he longed for the silent peace of a cloister, he put all personal desires aside simply because upon prudent counsel it became evident to him that his proper place was in the world.

An important meditation, the life of this ninth-century saint, for the modern layman seeking perfection in the world. For are not the same principles and virtues applicable to Catholic laymen in our very midst today?

St. Hedwig

There is a remarkable similarity between the life of St. Hedwig and her better-known niece, St. Elizabeth of Hungary (the latter's mother, Gertrude, was Hedwig's sister).

Both saints were child brides, wedded to noblemen of singular virtue as well as of great wealth. Both their husbands died prematurely. Both widows, moreover, lived as nuns, though neither actually took religious vows in a community.

The crosses each bore through life are also comparable, since in either case domestic strife was involved. Whereas Elizabeth's in-laws occasioned her much anguish, Hedwig's own children were principally to blame for her sorrows. (For some time, two sons, Henry and Conrad, took up arms against each other in a bitter dispute over property rights.)

Even St. Hedwig's self-chosen path to perfection parallels that followed by her niece a generation later. Thus, with Duke Henry's permission, Hedwig used castle funds to feed the hungry, care for the sick, succor the dying. One of her favorite projects was a hospital for women lepers at Neumarkt.

She went out of her way, too, in order to instruct the ignorant and encourage the wavering. Once she even made an elderly woman (whom she had chanced to meet) remain in the castle long enough to learn the Our Father properly.

After the Duke's death, Hedwig began to spend most of her days in a lodging near the Cistercian convent at Trebnitz, a foundation for which she had been chiefly responsible. There she worked, prayed, and performed penances along with the nuns, though she never became one of them. In this wise she remained free to administer the ducal estates in favor of the poor and the Church.

St. Hedwig died in 1243, and was buried at Trebnitz. In 1706, her feast was extended to the entire Western Church.

The longer the life of St. Hedwig is studied the more it becomes evident that the likeness between her and her niece, St. Elizabeth, is no mere accident of fate. Rather, Divine Providence was at work here. For the similarity functions to fix our attention upon the two women and to draw comparisons. As a result, God's message in their lives becomes clear: namely, that the sanctity of one generation is visited upon the next.

In this instance, St. Hedwig's goodness must have prompted the Almighty to shower special graces upon Elizabeth, a generation later. And largely because of St. Hedwig's intercession with God, Elizabeth remained strong enough to accept these graces and advance in holiness.

All of which means that the holier the family, the holier its offspring ought to be.

St. Helen ✠

St. Helen is best remembered for the role she played in the finding of the True Cross. Precisely what that part consisted of is not clear though. St. Cyril, who was bishop of Jerusalem shortly after her death in 330, failed to associate her specifically with the event. St. Jerome, who lived near Bethlehem not too many years afterward, was also silent about the connection. Yet Ambrose, preaching in 395, singled her out as responsible for the recovery of the wooden gibbet upon which the Savior died. St. John Chrysostom and several other later writers held the same.

When all the facts are considered, it is evident that St. Helen did make a pilgrimage to the Holy Land in order to supervise the construction of a basilica at the summit of Golgotha, in accordance with the wishes of her son, the Emperor Constantine. During the excavations there — Calvary had been profaned with pagan shrines by the Roman armies — the three crosses of Good Friday were uncovered, Christ's own still marked with the inscription citing Him as King of the Jews. Summoned to the site, St. Helen assumed possession of the sacred relic and took it upon herself to foster veneration to it throughout the world. Hence her name came to be especially associated with its recovery.

St. Helen is not ranked among the canonized simply because she was instrumental in finding the Holy Cross, of course. Rather it is because of her pursuit of perfection. This perfection was achieved at considerable effort, no doubt, for she was converted to the Faith only during her latter years (one historian claims she was 63 when baptized).

As a Christian, nonetheless, she lost no time advancing along the road to holiness. It appears that she chose self-abasement for love of Christ as her personal staff. Thus, she insisted upon attending Church services with the most lowly, dressing as simply as they, kneeling and praying with them. Her own fortunes she used partly for the sick and indigent, partly for the construction of basilicas and shrines, both at home and in Palestine. While sojourning in the Near East she even used her influence to free galley slaves and prisoners. "Though empress of the world and mistress of the empire," wrote Eusebius, "she looked upon herself as servant of the handmaids of Christ."

Nothing better typifies her self-assumed lowliness than the Sacred Wood with which she is forever associated. For the Cross is identified with Humility personified. Thus, in the epistle for the feast of the Finding of the True Cross, St. Paul observes that Christ made Himself as nothing, humbling Himself to the death of the cross.

St. Hilary of Poitiers ☩

Both St. Augustine and St. Jerome apparently borrowed from the writings of the fourth-century bishop, St. Hilary of Poitiers.

The West's champion of orthodoxy against Arianism, he was eventually banished by the Emperor Constantius, who had sided with the innovators. Undaunted, Hilary continued to attack the heretics from exile in Gaul. While there, he completed two monumental treatises. One, a twelve-volume work on the Blessed Trinity, scientifically demonstrated the divinity of Christ, the denial of which was implicit in Arianism.

No sooner had he been released, than he was in the midst of controversy again. For boldly upholding the decrees of Nicea, he was publicly styled the "Disturber of the East," and again exiled.

Following Constantius' death, he was back in civilization, beginning another crusade. This time he endeavored to rid Italy of its Arian-tainted bishops — a plan for which he soon drew the displeasure of the new emperor. Finally, however, under the guidance and protection of Pope Liberius, he dealt the heresy a fatal blow insofar as the Western Church was concerned. He died in 368.

A look into the background of a crusader such as St. Hilary is always interesting. In all probability, one might suspect he was trained in Catholic beliefs and fired with zeal from childhood.

Not so, however. The fact is that St. Hilary never saw the Church from inside until his adulthood. Born of pagan parents and reared in idolatry, his knowledge of Christianity derived from many long hours of study, profound thought, and humble prayer. Using his intellectual curiosity, he soon came to the realization that he was a free agent, composed not only of body but of an immortal spirit; created by God who was necessarily one, supreme, and eternal, before whom he must one day stand to be judged according to his virtues or evils. From the Old Testament he perfected his notion of God and morality. And, finally, in the New Testament he found Christ, the Eternal Word, in whom all truth is found and sealed. Having arrived at this stage, he had no alternative but to petition baptism.

But his quest did not end here. Being intellectually quick and a man of action, he could not be satisfied unless he dedicated his life to the defense and propagation of truth. Neither exile nor the prospect of death could stand in his way.

Thus St. Hilary typifies the militant convert who manifests his newfound faith through brilliant action, often putting lifelong Catholics to shame.

St. Hipparchus ✠

SS. Hipparchus and Philotheus are completely unknown to most modern-day Christians. So are five of their comrades: SS. James, Paregus, Abibus, Romanus, and Lollian. Together they are referred to by hagiographers as "The Seven Martyrs of Samosata," under which title they are commemorated each year.

The precise date of their martyrdom is given by some scholars as 297; by others as 308, or thereabouts. The first two named — Hipparchus and Philotheus — were

61

highly respected civic officials who had been baptized in their adulthood. Both of a zealous nature, they had succeeded in winning over the other five, all young patricians.

All these confessors appear in history for the first time when the Roman Caesar (either Galerius or Maximinus) proclaimed a special religious festival on the banks of the Euphrates, near Samosata.

The celebration was already in its third day when the emperor marked the conspicuous absence of the two magistrates. He accordingly directed that they be brought into his presence. When they flatly refused to take part in the idol worship, they were committed to dungeons. (Meanwhile their patrician converts were arrested and jailed.)

After the festival was over, the prisoners were interrogated once again, then racked, torn with scourges, and placed in solitary confinement. In two months' time, they were offered another opportunity to apostatize. For their refusal now they were condemned to the cross.

Seven gibbets were fixed near the city gates. Once again Hipparchus was ordered to worship the idols, and to persuade his comrades to do the same. Pointing to his thinning hair, the city father replied: "As this in the course of nature cannot be again covered with hair, so shall I never change and conform to your will. . . ."

Hipparchus was the first of the seven to expire. Three more were later impaled after they were hanged; and the remaining three barbarously ripped from their crosses and their heads pierced.

Heaven is secured, certainly, by any Christian who freely gives his life for the Faith. But when public officials — such as St. Hipparchus — or men of noble birth and learning — such as the patricians whom he converted — surrender their lives for Christ, the light of their example shines far and wide for countless men to see and follow.

When, on the other hand, prominent Christians apostatize or compromise their Faith, the sin is especially horrible. For their example then can only direct countless others — perhaps unknown thousands — to perdition.

The Holy Innocents ☩

"Childermas" was the name formerly given to the feast of the Holy Innocents. The feast, which dates from the fifth century, commemorates the martyrdom of the Infants of Bethlehem by King Herod.

Perhaps the most cruel tyrant of Jewish history, Herod heard that a "King of the Jews" had been born and, in his intense jealousy, vowed to slay the Infant. So, records St. Matthew, he assembled "all the chief priests and Scribes . . . and inquired of them where the Christ was to be born. And they said to him, 'In Bethlehem of Judea. . . .'"

It was then, continues the evangelist, that the Magi, learned men from the East, happened upon Herod's court in their own search for the newborn King. "Go and make careful inquiry concerning the child," the treacherous ruler said to them, "and when you have found him, bring me word, that I too may go and worship him."

But the Magi, warned in a dream of Herod's duplicity, never returned to the royal city. And on the word of an angel, Joseph took Mary and the Child by night into Egypt.

The awful massacre followed. Enraged because he had been crossed, Herod ordered that all male infants in Bethlehem and its environs be executed. To assure himself that the Christ would perish in the mass murder, he added the precaution: not only the newborn, but all males two years old or younger were to die.

The grief following Herod's nefarious butchery, notes St. Matthew, fulfilled the prophecy of Jeremias 600 years previous. Therein the prophet visualized Rachel, the wife of Jacob, weeping over the loss of her children from her grave: "A voice was heard in Rama, weeping and loud lamentation; Rachel weeping for her children, and she would not be comforted, because they are no more."

Just how many infants were cut down is not certain. Medieval legends place the number in the thousands, but a safe estimate, statistically speaking, would be much smaller. Bethlehem was a town of about 1000 inhabitants; thus the birth rate was probably around 30 infants a year. In view of the high mortality rate in the Orient, it is doubtful whether there were more than 25 victims.

Because they were the first ones to shed their blood for the King of Israel, the Holy Innocents were a type, as it were, of the thousands who have since gone to martyrdom vested in the white robes of innocence.

In a sense, too, they prefigured the countless innocent men, women, and children who are even today being slaughtered for the cause of peace, human dignity, and freedom, as, for example, the Hungarian infants who were gunned in their cribs by primitive Soviet madmen in our own time.

St. Homobonus ☩

Is it possible for a businessman to become a saint? None
but the most ignorant of the principles of holiness could
doubt for a moment that the answer is a loud yes.
Practically speaking though, in view of the multiple
spiritual dangers which are so closely associated with
business — occasions of sin as materialism, personal ambition, greed, injustice — has there ever been a successful
businessman who did attain perfection of soul? Once
again the reply is a strong affirmative. One example is
St. Homobonus (in Germany he is known as Gutman
— both words mean "good man").

He learned the clothing trade from his father, a
merchant of twelfth-century Cremona. From his father,
too, he received a solid introduction into the meaning
and importance of the virtues, and the need to strive for
personal perfection. Justice, honesty, and humility were
especially stressed, since they were the virtues most likely
to be violated in everyday buying, selling, and bartering.

Eventually opening up his own shop, he determined to
make it an instrument of sanctity. He looked upon his
work, one biographer notes, as an employment given
him by God.

As the years passed, Homobonus became one of the
wealthiest and most influential men in his community.
To conquer an ever increasing temptation to become
sophisticated, proud, and overly ambitious, he set out
upon a program of almsgiving, personally seeking out
the poor in their homes. And to purify his motives, he
fasted and prayed, never missing a daily visit to the
Blessed Sacrament in the Church of St. Giles, where
he also assisted at Matins and Mass. To show that his

motives were acceptable in heaven, God worked many miracles in his favor.

St. Homobonus died while attending Mass at St. Giles. The bishop of Cremona himself went to Rome to petition for his canonization, which Pope Innocent III decreed in 1199. St. Homobonus is today revered in certain localities as the patron of clothworkers.

The obvious lesson of his life? It is simply that a business, engaged in for material gain, is not necessarily ignoble. On the contrary, it can be very ennobling when pursued with supernatural motives. For then it becomes a ladder to holiness.

St. Ignatius of Laconi

St. Ignatius of Laconi lived the simple, uneventful life of a typical lay brother. During his first fifteen years in religion he worked silently around a loom. For the next forty years until his death, his chief assignment was begging food and alms for his fellow friars. Yet somewhere in the midst of his ordinary, insignificant duties, he managed to perfect his love for God to a heroic degree.

The island of Sardinia was his birthplace. His parents were very poor, but very holy — a contemporary described his family as a "household of saints." His mother, it seems, dedicated Ignatius at birth to God's service; she hoped he would someday become a Franciscan.

Her hope was realized. When Ignatius was 17, he fell seriously ill. Thereupon, he promised to become a

Franciscan if God would spare him. Upon recovery, he entered the Capuchin community at Cagliani.

Everything seemed to go wrong for him at first. His poor health was held against him. And an overzealous novice master called his sincerity into doubt. But somehow Ignatius was finally accepted and professed a Franciscan friar.

Then followed the fifteen years he spent in the weaving room. Perfectly resigned to the lowliness of his assignment, he offered up the hours he spent at it as acts of love to God.

In 1741 he was asked to leave the cloister in order to beg for the monastery. Now he had to knock on doors, meet strange people every day, endure the confusion and noises of the towns, suffer the ridicule and the questioning glances of passers-by. He had to condition his weak body to long periods of hunger and thirst, to sleeping on the ground, to walking hour after hour in sun and rain.

During these last forty years Ignatius grew to love God even more, despite the hectic life he lived. His time for contemplation was cut short by many distracting tasks, true; when he prayed, he prayed more perfectly than ever before.

St. Ignatius of Laconi died in his eightieth year, in 1781. His life represents a concrete answer to the confused worldly people who point to lay brothers today and ask cynically "But what do they do?" The reply: In the eyes of the world, usually nothing extraordinary; but in the eyes of God, to whom they have completely vowed themselves, enough to gain His very special love and to merit a high degree of eternal glory.

St. Ignatius Loyola ☩

As he knelt in the abbey of Montserrat that day in 1522
and hung his sword before our Lady's altar, St. Ignatius
of Loyola had no intention of renouncing knighthood.
Rather a new and greater legion he envisioned: a crack,
highly disciplined, expendable shock force dedicated to
the propagation of God's greater glory wherever it was
needed. It was a vision that he realized just twelve years
later, when the first members of the *Compania de Gesu*
gathered in the subterranean chancel of Notre Dame
on Montmartre and pledged themselves to God's service
by vows of poverty, chastity, and special obedience to
the Holy See.

Visitors to the Basque country of Spain can still see
proud Loyola castle where he was born in 1491. The
stately armorial insignia over the entrance still evidences
the noble military ancestry of his family, and indicates
quite clearly that he too must have been trained in the
knightly traditions of his forebears.

Ignatius held a command post in the royal armies until
he was cut down, seriously wounded, in the seige of
Pampeluna in 1521. A long convalescence literally forced
him to read, if only to while away the time; and among
the books on hand, providentially enough, were the Life
of Christ and the histories of SS. Dominic and Francis.
It was then that the idea of a great spiritual army began
to take form in his mind.

His health restored, the soldier departed, without his
sword, for the stark caves of lonely Manresa, where he
spent months in prayer and penance. From this retreat
came the outlines for his *Spiritual Exercises*, a manual
designed to effect the spiritual conversion of anyone
who seriously submits to it.

The rest of his life is common knowledge: how though in his thirties he studied for the priesthood, and enlisted his first recruits at the University of Paris (St. Francis Xavier was one of them); how he repudiated vicious calumnies and accusations of heresy to see his Society recognized as a major organization composed of well over a thousand members in his own lifetime.

Discipline and zeal for advance, both holdovers from his army days, characterized St. Ignatius' struggle for sanctity. Discipline, so manifest in his *Spiritual Exercises* demanding systematic prayer and mortification, and in his special vow of obedience. Zeal for advance, clearly marked by his motto, not a meaningless, sentimental watchword, but of itself a terrible challenge signaling that the task lies ever ahead; that there is no time for rest: "All for the greater glory of God."

Discipline and a passion for spiritual advance; are not these also the paramount devices of every militant Christian?

St. Isaac Jogues ✠

It will ever redound to the glory of the Jesuit Order that only the most brilliant of its ranks were deemed worthy enough to bring the Faith to the primitive Indians of seventeenth-century America. Those selected for the New World missions were marked not only by intellectual superiority and personal dynamism, but also by an intense zeal for souls and self-sanctification. One such missionary was St. Isaac Jogues.

He set sail from his native France shortly after ordination, in 1636. A few months later he joined a band of his fellow "black robes" who were already hard at work among the Hurons.

For six years Jogues preached to these barbarians amid the most foul conditions conceivable, but not without a measure of success. For the Hurons were less savage and nomadic than their Iroquois neighbors, and hence somewhat receptive to evangelization.

In 1642, Huronia was prostrated by epidemic and hunger. A relief expedition set off for Quebec, Jogues with it. René Goupil, a Jesuit lay assistant and a doctor, went too.

Blood-crazed Iroquois ambushed the party on its return and took them up the river to the shores of Lake Champlain.

With the others, Jogues was made to run the gauntlet. Pinned then to a post, his thumb was severed by a shell, his fingers were chewed to the bones, his flesh was seared a hundred times with flaming brands.

Death would have been merciful, but there was no death, at least not for the two Jesuits. Instead, they were made slaves to the Mohawks of Ossernenon (the present site of the Shrine of the North American Martyrs near Albany). Goupil was soon murdered, but Jogues groveled as an animal for 12 months before he escaped to France via Manhattan (he was the first priest to visit the island).

Back home, his mutilated features went first unrecognized by his very superiors. Queen Anne kissed his mangled fingers. And Rome gave him special permission to say Mass despite the condition of his hands.

1644 found him back in Ossernenon, this time as a peace ambassador for the French. After the treaty he returned, but his death was already decreed. A small box of religious articles he left behind in 1642 preyed upon the Indians' superstitious minds. The holy priest was tomahawked in September, 1646.

Ten years later Venerable Kateri Tekakwitha was born at Ossernenon. She was God's immediate reward for the Jesuits' having spared missioners of Jogues' caliber. The solid growth of the Faith in northeastern America is another.

The moral: when the finest of men make themselves most expendable for peoples whom the world considers the least of men, God is extremely pleased.

St. Isidore of Seville ✠

As a homeless, talentless boy whom nobody wanted, St. Isidore of Seville could hardly have dreamed that one day he would be the leading churchman in all his land. Nor could his tutors have guessed that this sensitive, listless youth who refused to study would achieve fame as one of the most renowned scholars of his time. Much less could anyone have predicted that he was destined to become a saint and a Doctor of the universal Church.

He was born around 560, the younger brother of St. Leander, the celebrated archbishop of Seville. Orphaned at an early age, he displayed none of the singular gifts of his older brother. He was slow in school, and like so many boys of his day and ours, often became lost on his way to class, on purpose.

Wandering through the countryside one day when he should have been in school, he became fascinated by a series of grooves cut by wet ropes into the stone walls of a well. If thin ropes could wear into thick rock, he thought, why could not similar constant application remedy his dullness in learning? He got to work.

The rest of his life reads like the typical success story.

Through hard work he soon became one of the most influential figures of his era. After the death of his brother, he was appointed bishop of the important See of Seville. As a scholar he perfected the educational system of his land and established a magnificent college. His writings represent the earliest chapter of Spanish literature. One of them, his *Etymologies*, was the most widely used college text of the times.

But his real success, of course, was in the life of grace. By applying the same principles of hard work to his spiritual life, he advanced so much in holiness that he was recognized as a saint by his contemporaries. He died in 636 in the Basilica of St. Vincent, lying on ashes and clad in a hair shirt.

The history of St. Isidore is the perfect success story, because his prize was the only lasting achievement, holiness. But more than that, his story is a stark reminder of what relentless effort will accomplish in the life of grace. Like temporal success, sanctity is the result of constant striving, like the wearing down of stone by the slow, steady friction of wet ropes.

St. Jean de Brebeuf ☩

Echon — "The man who carries the load" — is the name the Hurons gave Jean de Brebeuf when they saw him pick up a ponderous load of supplies and carry it unbent on a long portage through the Quebec forests. A giant of a man, who could match any Indian brave in stamina and prowess, he played the central role in the almost incredible story of the North American Martyrs.

Ordained but three years, he sailed from Dieppe in

1625. The following year he was already living with the savages of Ihonatiria, the nation bordering Lake Huron. He soon realized that his mission would demand extraordinary effort and God's special help.

The Indians acted as if they were only half human. They were vicious, treacherous, given to promiscuities and obscenities. They would torture victims for days amid cannibalistic orgies.

Living with the Indians was a nightmarish existence in itself. Their food was insipid, their cabins literally steeped in filth, crawling with vermin, overrun with rodents, permeated with a stench only flames could stifle.

Just when he was beginning to make some progress, war broke out between his country and England, and he was recalled to France. Before his return to Canada he wrote: "Lord Jesus, my Redeemer! You have redeemed me by Your blood. . . . That is why I promise to serve You all my life in the Society of Jesus. . . . I sign this promise in my blood, ready to sacrifice it all for You. . . ."

That sacrifice was called for in 1648, fifteen years after he arrived back in Ihonatiria. Just when the entire Huron nation was on the verge of conversion, the Iroquois went on the warpath.

Brébeuf was seized at one of his missions. Lashed to a stake, he was scorched with firebrands, his bones crushed, his flesh carved and eaten before his eyes. Because he would not cry out for pain, they tore away his lips and plunged white-hot irons into his throat. Then, in sacrilegious mockery, they "baptized" the priest in scalding water. After other revolting torments they scalped him, drank his blood, and tore out his valiant heart.

Whence this priest's valor? His love for Christ, of course, sealed in his vow of sacrifice. And the Pauline theme upon which he used to meditate daily: Who is there who can hurt you if you be zealous of the good?

St. Jean Vianney

The cynical question, "How does this man know letters?" voiced with reference to Christ in derision of His humble background, must have been repeated many times in the anticlerical circles of nineteenth-century France with reference to the Curé of Ars. Objectively speaking, there was cause. For only a moral miracle can explain how St. Jean Marie Vianney, today regarded as a patron of parish priests, ever completed his seminary studies.

Economic depression coupled with government instability (the Revolution of 1789) gutted France during his childhood, thereby intensifying the poverty of his devout parents. There was little time for school; he was needed in the fields to follow the plow.

Thus, Jean Marie was almost totally illiterate, when at the age of nineteen, he entered the seminary. Nor could he learn. He failed course after course, and was finally dropped. But where near-superhuman effort had fallen short, prayer and mortification won. Readmitted, he just about got through. But when he was ordained, eleven years later, there was one strange and humiliating restriction: he was temporarily denied permission to hear confessions, a right he did not obtain until a few years later, and after much coaching by the saintly Abbé Balley.

Ars, his initial assignment as Curé, was an uninteresting village of about fifty families, most of whom couldn't care less about the Faith. As he arrived there in the winter of 1818, his heart beat with one prayer: "Dear God, convert my parish." Nothing could change that prayer, neither man, nor hell itself.

Both tried; both failed. The villagers resented his stark preaching, his holiness of life. There were the usual rumors, lies, acts of hatred; one woman camped outside his rectory screaming insults. The devil fired his bed, set up a weird din the night long, whispered despair into his brain. In answer, the Curé prayed harder, ate and slept less, scourged himself longer, and preached the louder. And again God answered him.

Lines told him so, lines of penitents before his confessional, lines from Ars, from beyond Ars, from beyond France itself. For ten to sixteen hours a day, in the confessional, cramped, sweating, coughing a painful cough, until, at the age of seventy-three, he could hear the lines no longer. He wept because he could do no more. But Ars was again Catholic.

The Curé of Ars is a special patron for priests. But he is also the saint of the parish as such. His life is a clear proof of the relationship between a good parish and the Sacrament of Penance. For the busier the confessionals, the more crowded the Communion rails, whence comes the source of all Christian life.

St. Joan of Arc

The most fascinating, adventurous, marvelous, and mysterious chapter in the lives of the saints? Surely none comes to mind more swiftly than the story of St. Joan of Arc. It is also among the most tragic.

To the modern world her name resounds of heroic sanctity and patriotism, woven together into one unbelievably beautiful pattern. In her world, of course, her name was not so well accepted. Joan was much suspected by her own countrymen; taken for a witch by the English. Even when France finally had to face the horrible truth, promulgated from Rome shortly after her murder, that the Maid was innocent of all charges, a considerable segment of Gallican spokesmen still had doubts about her holiness. On the extreme side, cynics like Voltaire and Anatole France actually delighted in hurling foul insults against her memory. Even after her canonization in 1920, the campaign against her was still on. G. B. Shaw rejected the facts, and conceived of her as the first Protestant; another propagandist styled her as the earliest Feminist; and so on.

It is understandable, in a sense, that all manner of men might feel themselves qualified to offer opinions on St. Joan, for she belongs to secular history as well as to hagiography. But, in Browning's phrase, hers is "a history with a supernatural element, you know."

Her victory at Orleans in 1429 was only her first great miracle. Faithful to her Messire Saint Michel and the other heavenly Voices, the Maid soon cleared the road to the cathedral of Rheims, there to stand beside the Dauphin, to watch him enthroned as King Charles VII.

Charles was not near when Joan was captured by the Burgundians, however; nor when she was sold to the English. He remained cowardly silent during her long imprisonment, during the brutalities and indignities to which she was subjected. Nor was his voice heard in protest over Cauchon's unjust trial and her condemnation to the stake. So she died, at the stake, France's greatest liberator, before her twentieth birthday.

St. Joan was called by God, it has been said, to free her people from political chaos. The lesson? It is that whereas God ordinarily permits evils to exist in this world for our own spiritual betterment, He sometimes — rarely, though sometimes — takes extraordinary means to give peace, freedom, and happiness to a nation that has proved itself particularly loyal to Him.

As He did in France, He can do in modern Russia. A prayer to the Maid might very well hasten His action.

St. John the Baptist ☦

The miraculous events surrounding the birth of St. John the Baptist are related by St. Luke. The Angel Gabriel appeared to Zachary, while he was offering incense in the temple according to his priestly office, with the news that Elizabeth his wife was to bear a son, though she was far advanced in years. The boy was to be called John, the angel said, and was destined to convert a great part of Israel.

St. Luke also relates the story of the Visitation: how our Lady, informed by Gabriel that Elizabeth was to be a mother, went with haste to care for her cousin. When they met, St. John, though yet unborn, was cleansed of original sin, just as the angel had predicted.

While still a youth, St. John left his home for the southern deserts of Judea, where, alone, in fasting, prayer, and mortification, he prepared for his life's work: "to make ready the way of the Lord."

After long years of waiting, suddenly, in the fifteenth year of the reign of Tiberius, "the word God came to John." Thousands came to hear him speak of repentance for sin and were converted. Unlike other preachers of the time he repeatedly emphasized that he was only the Precursor of the Messias, whose shoes he was not worthy to untie. Faithful to his mission, St. John retreated into the shadows when the Messias finally appeared.

He died a martyr, the victim of the insane hatred of Herodias, whose adulterous union with Herod he had publicly denounced. When the king promised her daughter Salome anything she wished because the girl danced well, Herodias demanded John's head on a platter. Afterward, St. Jerome relates, she kept thrusting a dagger into his lifeless tongue.

The mission of St. John resembles, though to a lesser degree, the role of every militant Christian: *that Christ might increase*, as we decrease.

St. John the Almsgiver ✠

If "philanthropy" is a more acceptable term in modern society than "almsgiving," is it not because the former is more readily applied without reference to motivation?

A philanthropist need not involve himself in his projects; all that can be managed most efficiently by a board of experts. Nor need he act upon a reason which is truly spiritual. To be recognized as a philanthropist today, one need only to distribute his superfluous riches — a deed which is, after all, already incumbent upon him by virtue of natural equity.

The almsgiver, on the other hand, must acknowledge love of God as his basic motive. The very term is synonymous with charity — so the dictionary defines it.

All of which leads to one conclusion: if the word "almsgiver" is obsolescent, the cause must lie partially in the fact that there are few wealthy men today who give for the love of God — like St. John the Almsgiver.

A widower of known holiness, he found himself, at the age of fifty, elevated to the patriarchal throne of Alexandria in Egypt. Though the most illustrious see in the early Eastern Church, it was profoundly disturbed by a heresy which threatened to remain. To rid his diocese of this bitter strife, the new patriarch determined to resort to works of charity.

He began his offensive by giving away whatever remained of his own possessions. Then, with the offerings which continually poured into Alexandria's treasury, he helped feed, clothe, house, and care for the poor and abandoned.

He also used his tremendous influence in behalf of the impoverished and underprivileged. Because he was their advocate, no merchant or trader in the region dared overcharge them. Once he even prevented the governor from imposing an unjust tax.

St. John the Almsgiver died on Cyprus, the land of his birth, around the year 620.

His sanctity was occasioned, of course, by his almsgiving. But in more than the direct way. He realized, most vividly, that every poor person he aided in this life for love of Christ would return his help in the hereafter. Thus, he used to call the poor his "masters," explaining that they had great powers to help him when they entered paradise.

Help him they obviously did, with untold spiritual favors, as today's poor will surely assist those who assist them.

St. John the Apostle ✠

So sublime is St. John's Gospel that men will never be able, this side of eternity, fully to comprehend all the secrets it contains. Such is the unanimous verdict handed down from early Christian times by the greatest of saints and theologians. The breathtaking loftiness that characterizes the work could only have arisen from the incomparable sanctity of this Apostle.

He was called with his brother, James the Greater, as the two sat mending their nets by the sea. His father, Zebedee, was a prosperous Galilean fisherman; his mother, Salome, was one of the women who followed Christ to Calvary.

Though the youngest of the Twelve, John was chosen, along with Peter and James, to witness the Transfiguration, and later to accompany Christ into Gethsemane. With Peter he was assigned to make preparations for the Last Supper, during which he leaned upon the Savior's heart. Above all else, he was the only Apostle to stand with Mary beneath the Cross.

On Easter Sunday, John and the Prince of the Apostles were the first to arrive at the empty sepulcher. He was again at Peter's side when Christ appeared to test the latter's love.

After the Ascension, John continued to figure prominently in the acts of the Apostles. He was on hand when Peter cured the lame man in the temple. He took an active part in the historic Council of Jerusalem. And by all indications he was present at our Lady's passing — she probably stayed at his home during her final years.

Miraculously saved from a torturous martyrdom under

Domitian, St. John was banished to Patmos. Upon the emperor's demise he returned to Ephesus and finished his Gospel. With his death, about the year 100, the deposit of faith revealed by the Word Incarnate was terminated forever.

Every Christian ought to foster a very special love for St. John, for he was the one through whom the Savior gave us our Blessed Lady in those beautiful words spoken from the cross: "Woman, behold thy son," and, "Behold thy mother" (Jn 19:26). Hence "the disciple whom Jesus loved" was responsible for relaying Christ's most precious gift to man — His Immaculate Mother.

This is one reason, no doubt, why St. John's feast is so proximate to Christmas.

St. John Capistran ✠

"Small of body, withered, emaciated, nothing but skin and bone; but cheerful, strong, and strenuous in labor." Thus one contemporary describes the fifteenth-century friar, St. John Capistran.

A native of the Italian town of Capistrano, St. John became one of the most successful young lawyers of his time. Promoted to the governorship of Perugia, he increased his political prestige by wiping out local corruption and bribery. Then suddenly, in the midst of a promising career, he left the governor's mansion for a monastery.

His decision was occasioned by what might have turned into a tragic event. On a diplomatic mission to another region he was arrested and held captive. During his long imprisonment he began to think seriously about supernatural values and his soul. And upon his release from prison, he entered the Franciscan Order.

As a monk, his career was as brilliant as it had been in the world. He became known for his holiness of life, his prudence, and his eloquence as a preacher. He proved his ability as an administrator by thoroughly reforming the branch of Franciscans he headed.

His great influence on the fifteenth-century world is especially attested to by his work in the Crusades. When Mohammed II had taken Constantinople and was pressing hard upon Belgrade, the gateway to the West, St. John was instrumental in recruiting a veritable army to follow the Hungarian leader Janos Hunjadi.

When he died in 1476, the saint was seventy years old. Less than half of those years were spent in religion, but they were the ones which had begotten his real glory.

A vocation to God's service often seems to arrive at a time men judge inopportune. Such, some might have said, was the case of St. John Capistran. He had achieved initial worldly success, and was in the midst of what promised to be a prodigious legal and political career. Judging from his appearance, he must have fought against heavy odds to attain that success. To ask him to surrender what he had won with struggle and at so late a date would doubtless have seemed to his contemporaries the height of impracticality, too much for God to expect.

But God did ask, as He does today. And St. John did not hesitate. And the glory that became his for having reduced himself again to nothing is far greater and more lasting than the zenith of his earthly prestige could ever have been.

St. John Damascene   ✠

Syria was under the rule of a Mohammedan caliph throughout the lifetime of St. John Damascene, Doctor of the Church.

Oddly enough, the Christians of the seventh and eighth centuries were not overly oppressed by their infidel overlords. At least open acts of persecution were for the most part isolated, rarely part and parcel of a concerted campaign. St. John's father, for that matter, rose to become grand vizier of the government treasury without compromising his Faith. And the saint himself succeeded his father in the caliph's employ.

If John the elder had been a political appointee, though, his son could not have been better qualified for a revenue post. As a youth he had studied under a Sicilian monk (a war captive) who was particularly brilliant and learned.

It was precisely the memory of this monk's saintly example which soon occasioned St. John's resignation from public life and his withdrawal into the desert. For a retreat, he chose the monastery of St. Sabbas, near Jerusalem.

Ordained to the priesthood, St. John rapidly developed into one of the most effective polemical writers of his age. By force of circumstances, his principal target was Iconoclasm, the bitter heresy that rejected the use and cult of sacred images. It was the most deadly target at which he could have aimed.

For one thing, the Moslems, in whose territory he wrote his brilliant arguments, detested sacred images. The Jews were of a similar mind. And the Roman emperor, Leo the Isaurian, judged it expedient to propagate the heresy with torture and death. (He was sensitive to that fact that scores of Moslems and Jews served in his armies.)

For his forthrightness St. John was deprived of his right hand — he was spared martyrdom, in all probability, only because of his close ties with the caliph. But by the time the saint died in 749, the eventual death of Iconoclasm was a certainty.

Of all the details the liturgy recalls about St. John Damascene, his willingness to sacrifice his hand in order to promote truth and check error is given first place. An awful example, he, to that breed of men who decline to use their God-given talents in defense of truth for what they like to call "natural prudence," but which, in reality, is nothing other than sheer cowardice, perhaps betrayal.

St. John's hand remains ever a symbol of talent sacrificed for the love of the God who endowed that talent.

St. John Eudes   ☩

When beatifying St. John Eudes Pope Leo XIII referred to him as "the institutor of the liturgical *cultus* of the Sacred Heart of Jesus and the Holy Heart of Mary."

The saint was not, of course, the first person to preach this cult, for devotion to the Sacred Heart is as ancient as the Church itself. The early Fathers mention it in various ways: St. Augustine, St. John Chrysostom, St. Gregory the Great all dwell reverently upon it, especially in their commentaries about the piercing of the Savior's side with a lance (cf. Jn 19:34). Later on, St. Bonaventure, St. Bernard, and St. Gertrude — to name a few — were noted for their special devotion to the Sacred Heart.

Nor is John Eudes primarily responsible for bringing the cult to its present worldwide popularity. That was accomplished largely through one of his contemporaries: St. Margaret Mary Alacoque, an obscure Visitation nun.

But St. John was, in Pope Leo's words again, "the first to think — and that not without a divine inspiration — of rendering . . . liturgical worship" to the Sacred Heart, and veneration to the Immaculate Heart of Mary.

This devotion was the very keystone of his priestly activities. When he founded his Congregation of Jesus and Mary in 1643, he selected for its distinctive badge a representation of the two hearts fused into one. Under this insignia he preached over a hundred major missions, founded five seminaries, established his Sisters of the Good Shepherd.

Under this insignia, too, he published, in 1670, his *Devotions to the Adorable Heart of Jesus*, containing a Mass and a complete Office in honor of the Sacred Heart. The Office was first observed in one of his own seminaries shortly afterward.

His beautiful treatise on *The Admirable Heart of the Most Holy Mother of God* was finished just a month before his death. Previously, he had arranged for a feast in honor of the Immaculate Heart of Mary for his congregation.

St. John Eudes is an example of those few saints called upon by God to deliver a special message to the world. Because he was so chosen, there is a tendency on our part to argue for his greatness over other saints.

But is not the opposite more reasonable? The message, after all, is the important thing; the saint, but an instrument of God's will. In this respect, God's will was that liturgical devotion to the Sacred Heart of Jesus and the

Immaculate Heart of Mary should be fostered and spread throughout the world. That is a principal lesson we must glean from the life of St. John Eudes.

St. John of God

St. John of God is patron of the sick and of all who take care of the sick.

This saint was born in Portugal in 1495. When but eight years old he was kidnapped and taken far from home. He became a shepherd. Later he entered the army and fought in the ranks of the Emperor's mercenaries where he abandoned his Faith, forgot the moral law.

Then he fell seriously ill. This sobered him. He returned to the practice of religion and determined to live a saintly life in the service of the sick.

At first he nursed the mentally ill in an asylum. In every person, however confused or broken in mind, he saw the image of God, the presence of Christ.

Soon he decided on a hospital of his own, in Granada. He went through the streets seeking out the infirm, the diseased, the abandoned, and carried them to a few rooms he had rented. There he nursed them. To meet expenses, he hawked faggots of wood or begged from door to door. Startled, people regarded him as mad, but quickly came to see his heroic charity.

A few began to assist him, and, without his planning it, a religious community formed about him, the nucleus of the now famous Brothers Hospitallers of St. John of God.

His life was given to the service of the sick, and his death resulted from what he suffered in rescuing a man from drowning. As he passed into eternity, he gazed mutely at a crucifix, the symbol and summary of all he had sought to do and be.

His work continues today, not only in the institutions of his community, but wherever Catholics tend the sick, wherever there are Catholic hospitals, Catholic doctors and nurses. It lives in the tradition that this work is a sacred vocation.

St. John's ideal should be shared by all who take care of the sick. For as the Savior taught us, even a cup of cold water given to the thirsty in His name, is as something given to the Savior Himself.

John Nepomucene Neumann ☩

John Nepomucene Neumann succeeded Francis Patrick Kenrick as Bishop of Philadelphia in 1852, after the latter had been appointed to head the Archdiocese of Baltimore.

When he was informed of his nomination to the episcopate, Neumann tried every means in his power to decline. But Pope Pius IX was determined that he should accept. Thus Neumann arrived home one day to find on his desk an episcopal cross and ring: a sign that Archbishop Kenrick and stopped in to say that the Holy See would not waver in its original decision.

Bohemian by ancestry — Prachatitz was his birthplace — John Neumann studied at the seminary at Budweis and the University of Prague. He graduated from the university with high honors in 1835, at the age of 24.

His interest in America began, curiously, at Budweis. There he chanced to read a series of letters sent to the Leopold Missionary Society (the Leopoldin-Stiftung) by the great pioneer bishop, Frederick Baraga (a Slovenian immigrant who became an authority on several Indian tribes which he evangelized).

Though Neumann was not yet a priest, 1836 found him in the United States, where he was soon canonically adopted by New York's Bishop Dubois. Following ordination on June 25 of that year, he was sent to the missions of upper and western New York. Four years later he entered the Redemptorist order, and on January 16, 1842, became the first member of the congregation — founded in 1732 by St. Alphonse de Ligouri — to be professed in America. In 1847, he became a citizen of the United States.

For three years he served as superior of the Redemptorist house in Pittsburgh. When named the fourth bishop of Philadelphia he was serving as Provincial of the order.

His life as a bishop was relatively brief — only eight years — but his accomplishments were phenomenal. In 1852, Philadelphia had but two parochial schools: at the time of his death, there were almost one hundred. Fifty churches were built, and an ecclesiastical preparatory seminary was founded. To staff his schools and parishes he either helped confirm or newly introduced a host of religious communities: The Christian Brothers; the Sisters of St. Joseph, Notre Dame de Namur, Notre Dame of Munich, The Immaculate Heart of Mary, and so on. He also founded the first Italian parish, St. Mary Magdalen de Pazzi.

Bishop Neumann was one of the American prelates invited to Rome by Pius IX for the definition of the doctrine of the Immaculate Conception, and he was the first bishop in the United States to encourage the Forty Hours Devotion in his See.

As for his writings, they were especially solid. Among them, for example, were two catechisms, a Bible history, and a Latin manual explaining the Forty Hours Devotion. There were also his official works representative of his office: i.e., his letters to his flock, and the acts of the synods he conducted.

Despite his intense program of building, consolidating,

organizing and administering, the saintly bishop found time to carry on a personal missionary apostolate. He preached frequently, heard confessions, went on sick calls to anoint the dying. His confirmation schedule alone would have broken the health of many a man.

Though a scholar of distinction — he was not only proficient in theology but in some of the natural sciences as well — and an intelligent thinker, he mixed freely with his people, almost always speaking in their own tongues. He knew at least eight modern languages as well as several Slavic dialects, and when the Irish immigrants came to Philadelphia he learned Gaelic so that he could be closer to them. Many Irish immigrants who thronged to Pennsylvania during the potato famine of 1847 came from the hills of Western Ireland where English was not widely used.

Here is a bishop, then, who exemplifies several especially American characteristics: perseverance, solidity, an immigrant's courage, intellectual curiosity and, most obviously, care for people.

St. Joseph

In honoring St. Joseph, we are confronted with so long a list of virtues that we hardly know where to begin.

His name rings first of complete submission to the divine will. Because God said so, he took Mary to wife; there were no questions, not a moment's hesitation. At the word of the angel he rose in the middle of the night to set out for Egypt. And when he was told to return, he obeyed again.

He is the patron of patience, too. Though deputed by

God to watch over the Holy Family, he was never privileged to witness a miracle, nor the slightest public manifestation of the Christ Child's supernatural mission. Year after year, faithfully and quietly he waited, inwardly longing to see the first signs of the fulfillment of the prophecies he knew so well. He watched the Child grow stronger and learn to use the carpenter's tools, but died before the beginning of Christ's ministry.

He is also the saint of silence. Not a single word of his is recorded in Holy Writ. Besides, he is the model of humility, of prudence. And there are other virtues.

But the basic reason for honoring St. Joseph is his personal closeness to God. After our Blessed Lady no holier creature ever lived.

This, for two reasons. As foster father of the Incarnate Word, he was appointed to take the place of God the Father for a few short years and to be closely associated with the Son of God. Such a unique role joined him to God in a union which cannot be overshadowed save by that which unites Mary to the Child of her womb.

Second, his preeminent holiness arises from his association with Mary. To their marriage our Blessed Lady brought the most precious dowry a bride could present, the plenitude of grace. Pope Leo XIII says in his encyclical on the spouse of Mary: "Since St. Joseph was united to the Blessed Mother in the bonds of marriage, it cannot be doubted that he was closer than any other to this supereminent dignity by which the Mother of God surpasses so much all created natures."

It is for his personal holiness, his closeness to God, that the Church has placed him, after our Lady, above all the saints of heaven, and has declared time and time again, as the oppressed Hebrews of old said of their brother, "Go to Joseph."

St. Joseph Barsabbas ✠

Not long after the Ascension, St. Peter called together some of the first Christians for the purpose of naming a successor to the Iscariot, who had betrayed our Lord.

The minutes of the meeting are recorded in the opening chapter of the Acts. Two candidates were suggested for Judas' place: Joseph Barsabbas, surnamed the Just, and Matthias. After much deliberation and prayer, St. Matthias was chosen.

What of Joseph Barsabbas? Though largely forgotten by the faithful in general, he has been recognized by the Church as a saint.

He must have been of exceptional spiritual stature, otherwise he would not have been nominated for the apostolic college. St. Peter explicitly notes his loyalty to Christ from the very beginning of the Savior's mission. One ancient chronicler identifies him as one of the seventy-two disciples of the Lord. Papias says that Joseph eventually traveled throughout the world as a missionary, and that he once miraculously escaped death from poisoning, in fulfillment of our Lord's promise: ". . . if they drink any deadly thing, it shall not hurt them . . ." (Mk 16:18).

The details of his later life and death are unknown, although the *Roman Martyrology* does make the observation that he underwent persecution many times over before death.

The *Martyrology* also hints strongly at his dominant virtue — the one he undoubtedly relied upon above all others in his striving for perfection: namely, his absolute, unconditioned humility.

Despite the fact that he was openly passed over for

consideration as an Apostle, he nonetheless assumed an active role in the apostolate, burning himself out in missionary activity.

A vocation to the apostleship must, of course, originate with God. In itself, such a calling is a sign of God's special love. But it is not the only sign. There is a more basic, more vital vocation given by God to every man — the vocation to become a saint. Thus, St. Paul writes at the beginning of Ephesians: ". . . He chose us in him before the foundation of the world, that we should be holy and without blemish in his sight in love."

St. Joseph accepted his vocation to sanctity, and was humble enough to use his rejection from the apostleship as the stepping-stone to it. A similar rejection occurs at times among those apparently inclined to the priesthood or the religious life. In such instances, rejection is also meant by God as a means of meeting their fundamental calling to holiness.

The why of the matter is a divine mystery.

St. Justin

No Christian apologist of the second century surpassed the sharp-penned lay convert, St. Justin.

Known to history as Justin Martyr, he was born of pagan parents, near the ancient city of Sichem. Gifted with extraordinary acumen coupled with an insatiable thirst for knowledge, he literally spent his entire youth in traveling abroad in search of truth. At first he concentrated heavily upon the arts and physical sciences. But at length his ever searching mind set him on the quest for the ultimate principles only philosophy and theology can yield.

Epicurianism repelled him; Stoicism he reduced to nonsense; a peripatetic angered him; for the Pythagorean theorems he soon lost all patience.

Even Platonism failed to convince him, though it did occasion his conversion, at least indirectly. As Justin himself later admitted, his instructor in Platonic philosophy literally gave wings to his spirit, and he found himself drawn to a better knowledge of God. To this end he retired to a place of solitude at the seashore.

It was at the seashore that Justin chanced to meet a venerable old philosopher whose words fired him with a desire to read the Hebrew Scriptures and the New Testament writers, to check personally into the credentials of Jesus Christ, and to pray hard for divine guidance.

Once received into the Faith, Justin dedicated his remarkable talents to the defense of Christianity. Until his time, apologists had been generally content to refute the slanderous attacks made against the faithful.

But Justin lashed out in a new direction. His particular target, which he hit squarely again and again, was the juridical prejudice for which Christians were sentenced merely because they bore the name.

Three of Justin's polemical works have survived the ages: two apologies and his famed *Dialogue with Trypho*. For all their brilliance, however, they demonstrated far less, and were less convincing to the early Christians, than one single sentence he spoke as he stood trial for his own life. When asked to choose between apostasy or death, Justin clearly declared: "Nobody in his senses gives up truth for falsehood."

These words demonstrated to the second-century world that its greatest apologist died not merely for an ideal, but for a truth his penetrating mind had found and would not abandon.

So that St. Justin's death was really his finest argument. In recognition of this fact, the world has come to call him Justin Martyr, and not Justin Apologist.

There is no more convincing argument for the Faith than the willingness to die in defense of it.

St. Jutta

Jutta hardly sounds like a woman's name. At least the average American goes through life without ever having met a woman called by that name ("Judith" seems to be a close English equivalent). Jutta was a saint, nonetheless; a rather remarkable one. On the European continent she is a well-known saint, especially in Prussia, where she is venerated as a national patroness.

In many details, St. Jutta's history parallels that of her acknowledged model, St. Elizabeth of Hungary, who was born a few decades earlier. Both women were natives of Thuringia. Both were wedded in their teens to men of noble rank. Both were noted for their spirit of poverty and charity. Both were widowed early in marriage. Even the deaths of their respective spouses were alike: they fell victim to the plague on their way to the Holy Land, Louis of Bavaria for the crusades, Jutta's husband for a pilgrimage.

Alone with her children, St. Jutta saw each one of them enter the religious life before she herself set out on the path of spiritual perfection. First, she gave up her very last worldly possession to the poor. Then, donning a peasant's garb, she began to trek the Thuringian countryside doing whatever good she could: begging for food, for instance, to give it away to the destitute who were too sick to beg.

Her works of mercy finally took her far from her home into faraway Prussia, the land of the Teutonic Knights. There, with the permission of the Grand Master, a relative of hers, she retired to a solitary hermitage on the desolate banks of Kulmsee for contemplation and penance. Her particular intentions were the conversion of pagans and the perseverance of new converts. As a sign of His special love for her, God visited St. Jutta with visions and other supernatural favors.

Four years of intense self-sacrifice were all that her body could tolerate. Seized with a long and painful illness, she finally passed from this life in the year 1250.

Three things, St. Jutta was convinced, are capable of leading a person closer to God: a painful sickness, exile in a remote land, and poverty self-inflicted.

Not of themselves, however. For any one of them, experienced in an attitude of rebellion, is also capable of precipitating depression, even despair.

It is only when they are embraced willingly for love of God, as St. Jutta embraced them, that they inevitably occasion sanctity.

St. Lawrence ✠

The high altar of St. Lawrence Outside-the-Walls in Rome is by tradition reserved for the Pope alone to celebrate Mass. The historical reason is that this basilica is reckoned as one of the major churches of Christiandom; as such, it belongs to the world, not only to the city. In this there is a reminder of the spirit of its patron, a third-century martyr who left us an extraordinary example of the fact that the material possessions of the Church belong ultimately to all the faithful, especially the poor, who themselves constitute its most precious treasure.

August 10 is the date affixed to his account in the *Roman Martyrology*:

"At Rome, on the Tiburtine Way, the birthday of the blessed archdeacon Lawrence, a martyr during the persecution of Valerian. After much suffering from imprisonment, from scourging with whips set with iron or lead, from hot plates, he at last completed his martyrdom by being slowly consumed on an iron instrument made in the form of a gridiron. His body was buried by blessed Hippolytus and the priest Justin in the cemetery of Cyriaca, in the Argo Verano. . . ."

His exemplification of the basic principle of Church ownership occasioned his martyrdom. St. Ambrose gives us the details.

Archdeacon under Pope Sixtus II, St. Lawrence was in charge of all temporal affairs when the Edict of 258 inaugurated the eighth general persecution. Realizing that the Church would be forced to go underground and that its estate would surely be confiscated for pagan profit, he exchanged all ecclesiastical holdings for transferable goods and distributed them as alms to the poor.

When summoned before the Prefect of Rome and ordered to surrender the "treasures" of Christendom, he brought with him scores of destitute Christians whom he humbly announced: "Behold the treasures of the Church."

For this he was tortured, slowly at first, since he was still suspected of retaining hidden riches. But he had no other answer to give, so he was finally murdered, on a gridiron, in 258.

St. Lawrence's singular maneuver was undoubtedly permitted by God for a striking example that the temporal holdings of the Church, so necessary to her mission of channelling divine truth to mortal men, are only held in trust for the faithful whence they came to be.

The true treasures of the Church are the faithful, particularly the poor. For the poor are mostly Christians; and in the catalog of the saints, the majority, by far.

St. Lazarus

In one of Browning's most fascinating poems, Karshish the Arabian physician relates a strange medical experience. While traveling through Bethany he had met a remarkable Jew called Lazarus. "The man's own firm conviction," he writes in a letter to his home university, "rests that he was dead (in fact they buried him) . . . and then restored to life by a Nazarene physician" who called Himself God. No quack, this Lazarus, he apologizes, but an extraordinary personality, obviously motivated by a mysterious supernatural force; he seems to move in another world, to act as if he kept hearing again His master's word to "Rise."*

But suddenly Karshish cuts his epistle short. A human being returned from the dead? he asks in embarrassment. Impossible! Still, what if Lazarus were raised? What if the Nazarene physician were God?

The Nazarene, of course, was God, Our Lord and Savior Jesus Christ, and Lazarus of Bethany was actually brought back to life after lying four days in death.

* From *The Poems and Plays of Robert Browning* (New York: Modern Library Edition, Random House).

The details are recorded in the eleventh chapter of St. John's Gospel. There too the saint is identified as a special friend of our Lord's, and the brother of Mary Magdalen and Martha.

After the Ascension, reads a well-founded legend, Lazarus evangelized Cyprus, where, as bishop of Salonika, he worked for thirty years.

History attests to a widespread devotion to his honor as early as the fourth century. The Pilgrim Lady Etheria in her visit to Jerusalem around 390, for example, describes a procession on the Saturday before Palm Sunday to the Lazarium, where he was raised from the dead. Similar ceremonies were held in Milan on Passion Sunday ("Lazarus Sunday"), and in Africa on Palm Sunday morning. The many French shrines dedicated to St. Lazarus, incidentally, probably honor a fifth-century bishop of Marseilles, rather than the ancient saint of Bethany.

But, to get back to Karshish's letter in Browning's poem. Here is a case of an allegedly brilliant scientist coming face to face with a living miracle he had been taught to reject a priori. If he were really honest, he could have checked Lazarus' story through eyewitnesses, even through the Apostles who were still living. From a scholarly investigation, he could have proved the authenticity of the miracle, and the Nazarene's credentials beyond doubt.

Instead, when confronted with truth that seemed to contradict his "scientific" prejudice, he became a coward, an intellectual weakling.

The world is replete with men like Karshish. They would remain skeptics even if a new Lazarus emerged from the tomb every day before their very eyes, and if, like the Jews of old, they had the opportunity to talk personally to the God-Man who cured him.

St. Leo the Great ☩

Most of us remember St. Leo the Great as the pope
who checked the barbarians from overrunning Italy. His
meeting with Attila the Hun is one of those stories
found in almost every history book. But we know little
more about him.

He was of Tuscan lineage, but a Roman at heart.
There, in the city of Peter, he was born toward the close
of the fourth century; there he was schooled. There too,
in the service of several popes, he gained intimate knowledge of the work and the heartaches he was destined one
day to assume.

He was elected to the Chair of Peter in 440. Thereupon began one of the most glorious pontificates the
Church has known.

But it was not easy; his task was monumental. The
great Roman Empire, so closely allied to the Church,
was crumbling. The Emperor had already moved to
Ravenna, and the northern coast of Africa was in the
hands of the Vandals. From the north the Goths were
trampling over the last outposts of civilization with
blood and carnage. Attila and his Huns were eyeing for
conquest the beautiful valley of the Po.

The material ruin wrought by these barbarians did not
spell half the danger. Fanatics, all, they were steeped in
Arianism and other heresies that denied the very core
of Christianity: the Divinity of Christ, the Incarnation.
Wherever they roamed they spread these errors with the
sword.

More than once the heart of Pope Leo must have
been heavy. Who was he to withstand hordes of heretics
who threatened not only the Church, but all Western

civilization? But stand against them he must, else all would be lost.

His redoubt was the Rock of Peter. There, alone, he met the barbarians, not once, but again and again. And army after army reeled before the fortress upon which he stood.

In the midst of this international strife, he turned to the interior life of the Church. Reforms had to be made, the Rock had to be strengthened. Carefully he tightened administration, corrected abuses, checked dangerous innovations.

He died in 461, and was the first pope to be buried on the threshold of the Apostolic shrine. Here, even in death, he was to mount guard over the stronghold of the Prince of the Apostles.

It is good for us now and then to examine the lives of saints like Leo the Great in order that we may the more appreciate the present. Is not a similar situation to that of this era prevalent in the world today? Have we not now another saintly leader in the Chair of Peter? Will not the outcome of the modern struggle be the same?

St. Leonard of Port Maurice ✠

To the average layman, the "missionary priests" who preach parish missions present somewhat of a mystery. They seem to arrive from nowhere, remain just long enough to become known, then vanish as quickly as they came.

Their sudden appearance and disappearance can be

explained by the fact that they generally spend the major part of their days just preaching one mission after another. So ever changing and far-reaching are their assignments, that some rarely cross the same paths in a lifetime. And the brief respite they take from preaching, they spend largely in solitude, ordinarily in monasteries, preparing their sermons for the coming year.

Not that they are all gifted speakers. Oratorical talent, for that matter, is not essential to their apostolate. For the most successful "missionary priests" have frequently been mediocre speakers. They were successful because they were saints.

One example: St. Leonard of Port Maurice (so-called from the Riviera town in which he was born).

Ordained for the Franciscan Order in 1703, he spent close to fifty years directing missions and retreats throughout eighteenth-century Italy. So great were the crowds that came to hear him, he had to preach frequently in the open. In a typical encomium, one pastor attributed a remarkable change in his parish to Father Leonard's work. "God alone knows all the good he has done here," he said. "His preaching has touched everybody's heart."

His preaching? Or his holiness? The latter — about that, there is little doubt.

Because, first, he was a man of prayer. Countless hours of petition and meditation preceded every sermon he voiced.

Because he was also a man of penance. Though he almost died from the severe fasts he kept while a seminarian, still he continued to deny himself all but the absolute minimum of food for the rest of his life. He performed other harsh mortifications too, like taking the discipline. And regardless of the distance, weather, or his own health at the moment, he traveled to and from assignments on foot, until he was too feeble to walk any longer.

So that while his words may have been the proximate instruments of his conversions, the graces he occasioned for others were granted by God on account of his holiness. One clear proof: a group of English mariners were converted after listening to him speak despite the fact that they did not know Italian.

St. Leonard is certainly an exemplar for missionary preachers. But, by the same token, he is also a model for anyone who has ever made a mission or retreat. For conversions will not come principally through the priest's words, no matter how eloquent. They will come only through personal cooperation with God's graces, which are especially plentiful during a mission.

St. Lucy ☩

Dante Alighieri's special devotion to St. Lucy of Syracuse is clearly evidenced in his immortal *Divine Comedy*, wherein he speaks of her three distinct times, once to acknowledge himself as her "faithful one."

The reason, no doubt, for his predilection toward her was that she is the patroness of those afflicted with diseases of the eye or poor sight. Dante, it is known, suffered from partial blindness — this he candidly explains in his *Convivio*: "By overtaxing the eyes in a passion for books I so weakened my sight that the stars seemed in a kind of mist." So that the great Italian bard must have called upon her often while engulfed in those moments of sadness that try men faced with the real possibility of eventually going blind.

Just how St. Lucy came to be invoked against eye trouble is unknown, however. Probably it had something to do with the sound of her name. The Italian *Lucia* is very similar to *luce*, which is the Italian way of saying "light." And light, of course, is representative of sight, for it is sight's first object.

History cannot verify as absolutely certain the legend that her eyes were put out by a tyrant (or by herself to discourage an unworthy suitor), and later restored by a miracle. The familiar statue of St. Lucy holding her eyes upon a plate is undoubtedly based on such a legend.

The facts of her life are few and simple: she was a Sicilian, and she died for the Faith at Syracuse, around the turn of the third century.

According to the *Roman Martyrology*, she was delivered to profligates that her chastity might be insulted by her people; but, miraculously saved from this fate, she was first tortured, then "had a sword driven through her throat."

That she is one of the very few women saints listed in the ancient Gregorian missal is indicative of the extraordinary honor officially accorded her in the early Church. Her name still appears in the Canon of the Mass, and is thus mentioned a legion times daily throughout the world in the Holy Sacrifice.

In his *Commedia*, Dante makes St. Lucy the symbol of illuminating grace.

The metaphor is apt. For illuminating grace is that actual help by which God enlightens our minds to guide us heavenward — so much like the sight of our souls, therefore.

In this sense, St. Lucy should be able to claim each one of us as her "faithful one."

St. Luke ⚜

On or around his feast day on October 18 each year, members of the medical profession gather for the traditional "White Mass" in honor of their patron, St. Luke. The Mass is so named because white is symbolic of the garb worn by those who serve and heal the sick.

That the author of the third Gospel and the Acts of the Apostles was a doctor by profession is evident from several sources. St. Paul, in his letter to the Colossians, calls him "our most dear physician." In one of his most beautiful passages St. Jerome explains how Luke, the "physician of the body," became St. Luke, the "physician of the soul." In his Gospel the evangelist himself betrays his training by his constant use of clinical terms and medical phraseology, especially when describing the miracles of our divine Lord.

Though little is known of his youth, both the historian Eusebius and St. Jerome give his birthplace as Antioch of Syria. He was of the Hellenic world, then, probably a pagan. His excellent education is clearly attested to in his writings by his scholarly use of the Greek tongue.

The date of his conversion to Christianity is uncertain. It could not have been very early; for, as he himself admits in his Gospel prologue, he was not an eyewitness to the events of Christ's life. For his material he undoubtedly drew heavily on the already existing Gospels of SS. Matthew and Mark, and the oral and written catechesis of St. Peter and the Apostles. His beloved Christmas story he could have learned from our Blessed Lady.

The comrade of St. Paul during the historic missionary journeys, he remained with the great Apostle during his imprisonments and subsequent martyrdom in

Rome. Then, says legend, St. Luke set out to evangelize the Middle East.

He died, according to St. Jerome, at the age of 84, about A.D. 83, at Achaia.

The spiritual physician's mark is manifest throughout his Gospel, wherein he depicts the Messias as the Healer and Savior of the soul. Of all the evangelists, he alone, for example, gives us the stories of the lost sheep, the prodigal son, and the penitent thief. Again and again he keeps stressing the mercy and the love of the Divine Physician who goes out of His way to discover sick souls that He might heal them with His grace.

St. Luke is not only the doctor's saint. He is the one to invoke that God might continue to grant us health of body and soul.

St. Macarius

After having passed many years as a hermit in Egypt, St. Macarius was tempted to return to civilization and the active apostolate. He had the idea that he might like to dedicate the rest of his days to caring for the sick and dying in the hospitals of Rome. However, he suspected that his motives were a little wanting. And when he thought the matter over carefully, he concluded that his suspicions were well founded: all he wanted, really, was a bit of recognition for his life of self-sacrifice.

Try as he did, though, St. Macarius simply could not rid himself of this temptation by ordinary means. So early one morning he filled up two baskets of sand, balanced them upon his shoulders, and started a trek through the desert. When he was offered assistance by a passerby (who obviously was ignorant of what the baskets contained), he declined with the explanation: "I am tormenting my tormentor." That night, when he arrived back home, his peace of conscience was restored.

Once St. Macarius was asked to help decide what was to be done with a sum of money found in the cell of a deceased hermit. Some of the fathers were for giving it away. But Macarius, somewhat disturbed that a monk should have kept any funds for himself, and desirous of giving an object lesson to his disciples, ordered that the entire amount be buried with its owner.

On another occasion Macarius was crossing the Nile with some of his comrades, when they were observed by a group of military officers. The latter were overheard saying that the hermits appeared to be happy, despite their bitter povery. At this comment Macarius wheeled about and shouted out to the soldiers: "You have reason to call us happy, for this is our name. But if we are happy in despising the world, are not you miserable who live slaves to it?"

Just three examples, these, of literally hundreds of object lessons to be gleaned from the life of St. Macarius, who, in turn, is only one of countless desert fathers, who lived in the first few centuries. Though most of them, like St. Macarius, are little known and less understood, they all have important messages for modern man.

Just this brief reading about one of them, for instance, teaches us that: (1) some temptations are not overcome except by having recourse to extraordinary, even remarkable, means (though no one would be expected to carry sand bags through the city streets; (2) that hoarded riches might just as well be buried with the hoarder; and (3) the real slaves of this world are those who cannot comprehend the happiness of men who find freedom by rejecting the world.

St. Marcellus ✠

"Are you not ashamed to worship a man who was put to death and buried years ago by order of Pontius Pilate . . . ?" Thus the governor of the Egyptian Thebaid district began his frantic last-minute interrogation of St. Marcellus, a third-century martyr.

With the saint, sixteen other Christians, including his wife and two sons, stood in chains in the amphitheater at Thmuis, before the judgment seat of the ruler. In all their city, they alone refused to renounce Christ and offer sacrifice to pagan idols. For their staunch resistance they had already been condemned to die in the public arena.

But the governor, hoping to save face, had the prisoners dragged before him for one final inquisition. And in a desperate attempt to get them to reverse their decision, he made his sacrilegious remark about the Savior's ignominious death on Golgotha.

Clever though it may have seemed to the governor, the remark was neither original nor particularly pointed; it had been used a legion times by anti-Christians from the very beginning. And they had borrowed it not from one of their own number, but from the Apostle St. Paul, who had explicitly predicted that our Lord's crucifixion would be a "stumbling block" to many.

St. Marcellus and his companions refused even to acknowledge the governor's question. Instead, one of them made an open profession of faith in the divinity of Jesus Christ. After being exposed to various torments, the seventeen were then beheaded.

Like the third-century governor, there are still many men today who smile at, or openly mock, their fellowmen who insist upon believing in a Savior who died so lowly a death.

What such persons conveniently forget, or refuse to admit, is that the same Savior who died on the cross, rose from the tomb just as He predicted He would, in proof of His divinity. And that, like St. Marcellus and his companion martyrs, all who believe in His Resurrection will also rise to eternal glory.

In Christ's own words: "For this is the will of my Father who sent me, that whoever beholds the Son, and believes in him, shall have everlasting life, and I will raise him up on the last day."

St. Margaret of Hungary ☓

St. Margaret of Hungary is often confused with her compatriot, St. Elizabeth. The mix-up is readily understandable. Both women lived entirely within the thirteenth century. Both were daughters of kings. And both died prematurely, their bodies broken by heroic penances. There is this notable difference, however: whereas St. Elizabeth, the earlier of the two, was married and a mother, St. Margaret became a cloistered nun at an early age.

Hungary was being trampled by the Tartars when Margaret was born in 1242. To save his realm from destruction, her father, the indomitable and pious Bela IV, promised to dedicate his child to God's service. In fulfillment of that promise, and after the invaders had been driven from Hungary's soil, the king himself placed the princess in the hands of the Dominicans at Veszprem. A few years later he arranged for her transfer to a new convent, built as a gift to her, and located on the banks of the Danube, near Buda. There she made her religious profession.

As a nun, she decided upon a life of self-crucifixion. To compensate for an apparent deference shown her by the other Sisters because of her royal lineage, she deliberately sought out the most menial and revolting tasks, especially in caring for the diseased and dying.

During Lent she fasted and denied herself sleep to the limit of endurance. On Holy Thursday each year she insisted, by virtue of her prerogative as a princess, upon washing the feet of all the community Sisters and servants.

Her intense love for the poor and her sympathy for their hard lives found her catering to their needs at the least request.

She died at the age of twenty-eight, literally worn out by her austerities.

When Bela IV offered his daughter for the salvation of his nation, he never dreamed of the sufferings the princess would be asked to accept in return. But because she did accept them, according to God's will, his great nation escaped annihilation.

Today a new plea, equally as poignant, rises from the land of the Magyars. Once again that nation is on its knees and in chains.

Is it possible that St. Margaret is unaware of the present crisis? Is it possible that she who saved Hungary once will do nothing to preserve her people today?

But then, who has thought to ask her?

St. Maria Goretti ✠

Black headlines screamed the sickening story from Italy's newsstands that fateful evening in 1902; it went something like this:

Nettuno, July 5 — Alessandro Serenelli, the nineteen-year-old son of a tenant farmer here, plunged a dagger fourteen times into the body of eleven-year-old Maria Goretti this afternoon when the young girl resisted his advances. The victim, with whose family the Serenelli youth and his father boarded, was rushed by ambulance to a nearby hospital where she remains in critical condition.

The child died the next day, July 6, after forgiving her murderer. That date was chosen as her feast day when, just forty-eight years later, she was declared a saint by Pope Pius XII.

A modern-day St. Agnes, Maria grew up in the poverty and wretchedness of the Pontine Marsh district, south of Rome. When she was six her father brought the family to a village near Nettuno, in the hope of wresting a decent living from the reclaimed swamps there. But he suddenly died of malaria, leaving his wife Assunta and their six children penniless.

So Maria, though still a child, was charged with housekeeping, while her mother and the other children worked in the fields. They were thus employed the day Maria was attacked.

Alessandro was sentenced to thirty years' imprisonment for his brutal crime. During the trial it was learned he had made evil suggestions to the child before, but was firmly rebuffed. The last time he dragged, tortured, choked her, but her reply was final: "It is a sin. God does not want it."

The villagers of the Pontine Marsh could not forget that Maria had given her life in defense of her purity. Knowing that she must be in heaven, they began to invoke her. And many of their prayers were answered with miracles: a tubercular was cured instantly; a crippled war refugee who crawled to her casket was healed.

And Alessandro himself was converted. Upon leaving prison (where Maria appeared to him once) he begged Assunta's pardon. He obtained permission to serve as a caretaker in a monastery to make reparation for his crime. He even testified to Maria's sanctity before Church authorities.

Present at Maria's canonization in 1950 were her mother, then in her eighty-eighth year; her two sisters, and her brother.

With the high incidence of sex crimes in America today, Maria Goretti is a twofold patroness, as the father of a recent victim has pointed out. First, as a real model of purity for youth. And, second, as the heavenly refuge of those who are guilty of such foul crimes.

St. Mark ☩

A convert of St. Peter whom he later served as secretary, St. Mark is immediately recognized as the evangelist, the author of the second Gospel. He is also revered by the Church as a martyr, and, according to a tradition traced to the historian Eusebius and confirmed by St. Jerome, the founder of the Church at Alexandria in Egypt.

The first scriptural indication as to the identity of St. Mark, or "John Mark" as he is sometimes called, occurs in the twelfth chapter of the Acts of the Apostles. There reference is made to a home in Jerusalem owned by his mother Mary, in which the early Christians were accustomed to gather. St. Peter fled to this place after his miraculous escape from the dungeons of Herod Agrippa.

St. Mark's initial years as a Christian were spent almost entirely in intense missionary activity. Inflamed with zeal for souls, he accompanied his cousin St. Barnabas and the great Apostle St. Paul on their first journey. Later he and St. Barnabas set out to evangelize Cyprus. Returning to the West, he visited St. Paul before the latter was martyred, then embarked for new missionary conquests in the East.

That he was closely associated with St. Peter is certain. Papias, a first century writer, asserts that St. Mark was a "disciple and interpreter" of the first Pope. From the Prince of the Apostles he doubtless obtained many of the details narrated in his work.

His death is described in the *Roman Martyrology*: "Arrested for the faith, he was bound, dragged over stones, and endured great afflictions. Finally he was imprisoned, where, being comforted by the visit of an angel, and even an apparition of our Lord Himself, he was called to the heavenly kingdom in the eighth year of the reign of Nero."

Although we usually think of him first as the evangelist, St. Mark is really the perfect example of the missioner. For years he traveled in foreign lands, enduring hardship and hatred, to bring Christ's love to unfortunate men. Under divine inspiration, he recorded that love in his Gospel, that generations in the future might know and experience it. And lest his missionary spirit be wanting in the slightest, he sealed his Gospel with his own blood.

St. Martin of Tours ✠

Our English word "chapel" is derived, surprisingly enough, from the historic cloak (*chapele, in Old French*) of St. Martin of Tours. According to the *Oxford Dictionary*, the term was first applied to the shrine or sanctuary in which his cloak was preserved. Gradually *chapele* came to be a synonym for all lesser sanctuaries which were not churches.

That cloak was the portion of the military cape Martin gave away one winter to a beggar at the gates of Amiens. Slashing it in two with his campaign sword, he gave half of it to the shivering old man, then stormed away amid the taunts of his pagan comrades. That night Christ Himself appeared to the conscientious young legionnaire in a dream. Our Savior was wearing the beggar's half of the cape, and He said: "Martin, yet a catechumen, has covered Me with this garment."

After this vision, the youth was baptized, resigned his commission in Julian's mercenaries, and set out on the road to sainthood. First on his agenda as a new Christian was the conversion of his mother and family. Next he turned his efforts toward his own sanctification.

Ordained an exorcist by St. Hilary of Poitiers, under whom he had studied, he retired from the world for solitary prayer and penance. But his reputation as a mystic spread, and soon a band of hermits sought his direction. Together they built the great cloister of Ligugé, traditionally recognized as the first true monastery in Gaul.

Elected bishop of Tours in 371, Martin refused to mitigate his stark personal life. For his residence he chose Marmoutier, then a desolate retreat on the banks of the Loire. From there he ruled his see.

At Marmoutier he founded a monastery that was to attract some of the greatest saints and scholars of the age. Each year he traversed every corner of his diocese, preaching, administering the sacraments, refuting pagans and heretics, and working countless miracles.

St. Martin is the type of the militant Catholic, whether he be bishop, priest, or layman; the kind of Catholic who cannot breathe unless he is preaching God to his fellowmen. His life fulfilled the words of the Gospel: "No one lights a lamp and puts it in a cellar or even under the measure, but upon the lamp-stand, that they who enter in may see the light." Should we not all do likewise with the light of faith?

The Martyrs Under Nero ☩

In trying to explain away the miraculous nature of the Church's growth during the first few decades after its institution, certain social historians have fabricated some rather amazing, though worthless, theories. For the phenomenal rise of Christianity is absolutely inexplicable unless one accepts the premise that the finger of God was there in a special manner. The awful ordeals to which the earliest faithful were subjected for their belief in Christ clearly testify to this fact. In particular, one has but to recall the first imperial persecution under Nero, from 64 to 69. The countless martyrs of these years are commemorated on June 24.

In the summer of 64 — hardly a generation after Christ had commissioned His Apostles to preach to all nations — a devastating fire began to rage out of control in Rome. For almost a week it roared, gutting two thirds of the city. On about the third day, Nero appeared atop the Tower of Maecenas, where, costumed like a Greek tragedian, he recited Priam's Lament while playing upon his lyre. So sadistic a delight did he take in the flaming scene that the rumor was quickly passed that he himself had ordered the holocaust.

To stifle such talk, records Tacitus, who was eyewitness to the events, "Nero falsely accused and punished with the most fearful tortures the persons commonly called Christians. . . . Made the object of sport, [they] were covered with the hides of wild beasts, and tormented to death by vicious dogs; or else they were nailed to crosses, or even set afire, and when the day began to wane, were burned to serve as night lamps. Nero offered his own garden for the spectacle . . . mingling with the common people in the dress of a charioteer."

The death toll of this first Roman persecution is not known. It is certain that it was very large. And given the relative infancy of the Church, it was surely tantamount to a decimation, at least. It ceased only with Nero's self-murder in 69.

Despite the horror of it, Nero's persecution sounds a note of optimism for the horrors of the present day. For if it was impossible for the Roman Emperor to crush out Christianity when the faithful were but a few, and the whole world not only Roman but, except for a small section, profoundly pagan, how much of a dent can the Communistic machine and its allied forces make in the walls of the Church now?

The Martyrs of Uganda ✠

Not too many American Catholics, it seems, could name "the martyrs of Uganda," or, for that matter, just explain the phrase. For relatively few people in this country possess more than but a passing acquaintance with the history of Christianity in interior Africa.

Such ignorance is particularly unfortunate because as His Holiness Pope Pius XII stressed in his encyclical, "The Gift of Faith," the African Church is rapidly attaining a position of world significance. And the record of its recent growth cannot be unfolded without constant reference to the remarkable native converts who shed their blood there for the Faith. Typical of them were Joseph Mukasa, and Charles Lwanga, two of the twenty-two Bantus who are commemorated as "the martyrs of Uganda."

When the intrepid White Fathers established their first missions among the Buganda tribes around 1879, they were received with favor by the supreme chieftain. With the succession of King Mwanga a few years later, however, the atmosphere became tense. Wily and thoroughly immoral, the new monarch despised Christians with a bitter hatred, one that was continually fed by lies propagated by Arab traders.

Mwanga's first violent act of persecution occurred in 1885. Joseph Mukasa, a newly baptized native assigned to the royal dwelling, lashed out against his ruler's debauchery, his corrupting influence over the village youths, and his part in the recent slaughter of a Protestant minister and his retinue. In reprisal, Mukasa was summarily slain.

His murder fired further secret conversions, especially among the youth Mwanga had hopes of perverting. When the king learned of this, he flew into a rage, hurling a spear through the throat of an innocent boy. Then, barring all escape from the village, he summoned his subjects and gave them each the choice between Christianity or death. Seventeen youths, led by Charles Lwanga, stepped forward and shouted, "Till death!"

Condemned to die, the band was led far into the

jungles, to a place near Namugongo. One was savagely cut down on the way; another, before the actual ordeal of torture began. The rest were bound in faggots and burned alive.

A year later, 500 of the Buganda people had received baptism, and over 3000 were preparing for it. So the fires of Namugongo were not set in vain, for they illumined the Dark Continent with light drawn from the Eternal Sun.

Dramatically, the martyrs of Uganda exemplify what Christ asked every one of His own to be — "the light of the world" that "gives light to all."

St. Martin de Porres ☩

By popular acclaim the patron of interracial justice in the Americas, St. Martin de Porres is probably best known for his amazing charisms.

His miracles, above all else: his multiplications of food for instance, or the many instantaneous cures he wrought.

Bilocation, too. He never left seventeenth-century Peru; yet he was seen more than once in distant parts of the world by South American merchants in their travels abroad.

Like St. Francis of Assisi, he also found no problem in conversing with birds and animals. Once he even ordered a whole army of pestiferous rodents out of the monastery into an unused shed. Apparently he did not lead them out as Browning's Pied Piper of Hamelin did two centuries after.

The sanctity of this remarkable Dominican lay Brother

was not based upon these supernatural gifts, however, but upon the heroic virtue he practiced.

Inside the monastery, he made himself a slave to the other monks. He was everything to them: infirmarian, launderer, cook, porter, janitor, procurator, barber. In each role he expended himself to the limit of endurance for the love of God.

Outside the cloister, he was equally the slave. He roamed the streets in search of the poor, sick, and dying, bringing them food and medicine; remaining with those about to live through their last agony. For the countless abandoned infants and children of the city he established a foundling home and an orphanage. And all, again, for the love of God.

If Brother Martin was a half-caste, none of his people even noticed. They did notice that he was holy. So they flocked to him for his counsel and for his benediction.

But the veneration of an entire continent could not have shaken the profound humility of this simple lay Brother. On one occasion he offered to sell himself into servitude to free his monastery from serious debt. "I am only a poor mulatto," he said. "Sell me."

Yet when this poor mulatto died in 1639, high-ranking prelates and nobles bore his body to the grave. To them he was a prince among men, for he was surely one of God's closest friends.

If St. Martin the mulatto was one of God's friends, how friendly to God can those men be who would refuse him a seat in a bus, or a table in a restaurant, were he living in their midst today?

St. Mary Cleophas   ✠

Besides our Blessed Lady and St. John, a small group of women kept vigil at the summit of Calvary, as Christ the Eternal Lamb poured forth His precious blood for the redemption of the race. One of them was St. Mary of Cleophas. So says the beloved Apostle in his Gospel: "Now there were standing by the cross of Jesus his mother and his mother's sister, Mary of Cleophas, and Mary Magdalene" (19:25).

From St. John's description it is not clear whether the phrase "his mother's sister" refers to Mary of Cleophas or to a fourth woman.

Down through the centuries there has been considerable discussion on this point. Those who have held the latter view have generally identified the unnamed woman with St. John's mother, Salome, whom St. Mark explicitly mentions in his Crucifixion scene. But those who have maintained that the words "his mother's sister" mean that the wife of Cleophas was our Lady's full sister, have found it difficult to produce convincing arguments for the likelihood that the two sisters would have had the same name.

It is quite possible that Mary of Cleophas was really the sister-in-law of the Blessed Virgin. For according to the second-century historian Hegesippus, Cleophas was actually the blood brother of St. Joseph, and two of his sons, referred to elsewhere in Scripture, were known as the "brethren" (i. e., cousins) of Christ.

Outside of such brief reference in the Gospel, nothing is known for certain about St. Mary of Cleophas. A complicated framework of legends, however, identifies her as the Mary who accompanied Lazarus to Provence, and there is an immemorial belief that her body is buried in the vicinity of Saintes-Marie, near the mouth of the Rhone.

The only important fact about her life, however, is that she stood with our Lady beneath the cross of Jesus. The secret of her message to the world must be contained somewhere in this privilege.

It would seem, for one thing, that she was so privileged to gain merit for her illustrious son, St. James the Less, who was to become the first bishop of the Jerusalem of the New Testament sealed at Golgotha. By the divine will he was destined to become the first high priest of the newly redeemed sacred city. Yet he perished by the hands of those whom he tried to save, all the time praying the same prayer his mother heard from the cross: "Father forgive them, for they do not know what they are doing."

St. Mary Euphrasia ☒

Histories of religious foundresses usually have little popular appeal. St. Mary Euphrasia Pelletier is somewhat of an exception. It may be true that her name is almost totally unfamiliar to the average Catholic. But there is hardly an informed person anywhere in the world today who would not be ashamed to plead ignorance concerning the brilliant community for which she was responsible: the Institute of Our Lady of Charity of the Good Shepherd — the "Good Shepherd Sisters."

At Tours, in 1814, while still in her teens, she was received into the novitiate of the famed Convent of the Refuge, an institution for women established by St. John

Eudes almost two centuries earlier. Named superior in eleven short years, she soon found herself in charge of a new convent at Angers.

The rest of her story is that of a saintly, highly sensitive soul sacrificing her final measure of strength to preserve and give new life to an apostolate which few persons really understood, many obviously did not want, very many suspected, and practically none appreciated.

The issue about which most of the controversy characterizing her life developed was her unconditional insistence upon a centralized organization for the Good Shepherd Sisters. The older concept allowing for autonomous Houses of Refuge for women, she was thoroughly convinced, was gravely prejudicial to the work of the Sisters. So that despite the heartache and the bitterness which great controversies inevitably occasion, Mother Euphrasia pressed ever for the stand she felt to be the only right one — an attitude that must have meant living martyrdom for a woman so keen of soul.

And she won the day. What was in effect a new institute, that "of the Good Shepherd," soon arose at Angers. Papal approbation was not long in coming.

The proof of Mother Euphrasia's good sense as well as her sanctity (for the two must be wedded in a foundress) is evident from the fact that when she died in 1864, the Good Shepherd Sisters numbered close to 2760 throughout the world.

But to return to our original point. How is it that the life of this particular nun can have practical meaning for nonreligious living in the world?

The answer lies not in her mode of action, but in her motivation. Only one principle guided this woman's life every moment of the day. No matter how awful the struggle, or how hopeless the outlook, she never lost sight of a phrase St. John Eudes himself had spoken to his Sisters: "Remember that a soul is worth more than a world. . . ."

Now who of us cannot learn from this woman?

St. Matthias ☒

St. Matthias is often confused with St. Matthew, the author of the first Gospel. Both were Apostles. But St. Matthias did not become one of the Twelve until after the Crucifixion. He it was who took the place forfeited by Judas.

The only facts we know about his life are recorded briefly in the first chapter of the Acts of the Apostles. Following the death of the traitor, St. Peter called the disciples together for the purpose of bringing the number of the elect again to twelve. "And they put forward two," Scripture says, "Joseph called Barsabbas . . . and Matthias."

Then they prayed: "Thou, Lord, who knowest the hearts of all, show which of these two thou hast chosen to take the place in this ministry and apostleship from which Judas fell away to go to his own place. And they drew lots between them, and the lot fell upon Matthias; and he was numbered with the eleven apostles."

Nothing more of St. Matthias is known with certainty, although he is mentioned frequently in early apocryphal writings. One legend describes his martyrdom at the hands of Ethiopian savages. Another pictures him as a victim of stoning within the walls of Jerusalem.

Yet the brief passage in the Acts provides us, as does every paragraph of Sacred Writ, with the basis for deep theological speculation. His short history is really a pointed sermon on the true nature of a vocation to the priesthood.

Mark the circumstances of his election to the apostolate. Both he and Barsabbas were nominated as candidates for the ministry; evidently both were eminently acceptable in sanctity and in talent.

But the final decision was God's. The disciples knew it; that is why they prayed. They knew that, out of the many who are acceptable, for His own reasons God chooses only some.

A vocation is truly a divine gift. No human being could possibly be worthy of it, could ever merit it.

In Hebrew the name Matthias means "a gift of God." Very apt.

St. Maurice ☒

The martyrdom of St. Maurice and his comrades of the Theban Legion has surely been related a thousand times and in a thousand ways. The very phrase, "St. Maurice and the Theban Legion," has long been a familiar one, a symbol of soldierly loyalty to God and country.

Around the year 287, the Theban Legion, whose members were for the greater part Egyptian Christians, was ordered to proceed to what is now Switzerland, there to meet with several other legions along the Rhone. The insurgents, from all indications, were the Bagaudae, a Gallic people. (The allegation that this particular campaign was organized for the persecution of Christians seems unfounded.)

Rendezvousing before the opening battle, all officers and men were commanded to join in asking the gods

123

of Rome for a quick victory. Immediately, St. Maurice protested. To emphasize his stand, he led some of his troops from camp to a nearby spot, presently known as St. Maurice-enValais. There the group awaited judgment one way or the other.

Decimation was then decreed by the commander in chief of the combined imperial forces. Each tenth man of Maurice's troops, chosen by lot, was slain. When the survivors of this first slaughter remained steadfast in their refusal to participate in pagan rites, a second decimation followed. Finally, those who were still alive were cruelly cut down, their armor and weapons divided as spoils. Strengthened in soul by such bravery, several other legionnaires openly declared their loyalty to Christ, and were likewise slain.

The exact number who died with St. Maurice is not known for certain. It is amost inconceivable, however, that an entire legion (which could have included over six thousand men) was involved. In all probability, but a small percentage of the Theban unit was slain; perhaps, only a squad.

St. Maurice, as one might expect, is widely venerated as the patron of infantry soldiers. The precise reason for this can be found in the martyr's own words, recorded, at least in substance, by a fifth-century writer who cited eyewitness accounts as his source of information. Thus, when accused of insubordination and disobedience for his refusal to honor false gods, Maurice replied for himself and for his men:

"We have taken an oath to God before we took one to you: you can place no confidence in our second oath if we violate the first."

Loyalty to one's human superiors rests, in other words, on one's belief in, and love for, God. No oath has force without reference to God.

St. Maximus ☨

An octogenarian martyr, St. Maximus, was as fearless as he was eloquent in defense of the Faith.

For refusing to remain silent in the face of grave theological errors, his tongue and his right hand were taken from him. He was then paraded through the streets of Constantinople locked in a pillory. Finally, he was shipped off to the bleak shores of the Black Sea, and there abandoned to perish from hunger and the cold.

The courageous old man died a few weeks later, in 662. And not really disgraced or broken, either; but like the conqueror capturing the prize. For by the grace of God he had succeeded in living up to the principle he had so boldly enunciated at the time of his very first trial: ". . . I would rather lose my life than depart from the least point of the Faith."

Heresy, not paganism, occasioned his martyrdom. Monotheletism was its name.

A preposterous theological system ultimately leading to a denial of Christ's humanity, this heresy was invented by a faction of overly compromising Churchmen who hoped thereby to bring Egypt back into the unity of the Faith. That nation had previously espoused another crude heresy, which was almost immediately condemned by the Holy See. Still smarting under the Roman censure, the proud Egyptians were on the verge of divorcing themselves from the empire, politically as well as spiritually.

From the imperial palace, Heraclius quickly threw his influence behind the new heresy, lest the Egyptians follow through with their threat.

St. Maximus, then the first secretary at the palace

court, countered by resigning in protest. Entering a monastery, he then began preparing himself for the terrible fight he knew must come, and one which he felt he might be destined to spearhead.

Battle was joined under the new ruler, Constans II. To force the heresy on all his subjects, he even exiled Pope St. Martin I, who died of maltreatment as the last martyred pope. Then the emperor turned upon St. Maximus. The remaining details of the saint's life are those of his imprisonment, exile, torture, and death.

What can we glean from the life of St. Maximus? This: that heresy is really quite an ugly thing, an evil we must condemn even at the risk of death. It matters not what form heresy assumes; whether it attacks the sacred humanity of Christ, as did Monotheletism of old, for instance; or whether it rejects His divinity, as do some sects today. Our attitude must still be that, and only that, of the saint:

"I would rather lose my life than depart from the least point of the Faith."

St. Melchiades　　✠

One of the three Negro popes generally acknowledged by chroniclers of the papacy was St. Melchiades (or Miltiades).

Generally, we say, because it is not absolutely certain that all three pontiffs were members of the Negro race as such. Chances are, moreover, that the matter will never be crystal-clear.

First, because early Christian historians were evidently not concerned about the fact of a man's color, and hence rarely saw any good reason for recording such

126

intelligence.

Also because of the fine line anthropologists and ethnologists draw between the true Negro race and the various Negroid races, which even in early times were spread throughout the Dark Continent.

And finally, because fourth-century North Africa, from which St. Melchiades came, was the homeland of Hamitic peoples who ranged widely in skin color.

Despite such historical and scientific difficulties, however, many modern scholars are agreed that if the three so-called Negro popes were to appear in certain sections of our own country today they would surely be subject to racial bias on account of their color.

St. Melchiades, the second of the three chronologically, ascended the Chair of Peter in 311, just a year before the General Persecutions came to an end.

His signal mark on history was made in connection with the trial of a North African bishop, whose episcopal orders had been impugned by a heretical group that threatened the sacramental system of the Church. St. Melchiades was instrumental in disproving the charges against the bishop and, at the same time, in blunting, at least temporarily, the initial offensive of the heresy (called Donatism). For his leadership during the episode, so painful to a Church just arisen from the catacombs, the Pope was cited by St. Augustine as "a great son of peace, a true father of Christians."

St. Melchiades died in 314 and was buried, it is thought, in the cemetery of Callistus, on the Appian Way. He is mentioned in the *Roman Martyrology* on December 10, because of the sufferings he endured for the Faith prior to his election to the papacy.

The thought of a Negro being the Father of all Christendom, the successor of St. Peter, and the Vicar of Christ on earth, might seem remarkable to certain individuals in our own nation who would refuse to receive the sacraments from a priest of Negro blood.

But the thought was obviously not out of the ordinary to the early Christians. Nor to God, who accepted this particular Pope as one of His very special friends.

St. Monica ✠

When first she learned of her son's departure for the pagan centers of Rome and Milan, St. Monica must have wept in sorrow. All her prayers for his conversion suddenly seemed in vain, all her hopes dashed. In her grief she could hardly have realized that God had already begun to answer her petition. For it was in Milan that her son Augustine was to discover God and the road to sanctity.

St. Monica was born around 333, most probably at Tagaste, in North Africa. Her parents were both Christian, though there is evidence of some laxity on their part. For one thing, her religious education was left to a servant. More surprisingly, she was given in marriage to a pagan, a man by the name of Patricius. At the time she was only seventeen; he, middle-aged.

Her greatest cross, however, was her eldest son, Augustine. It frightened her to watch him grow to imitate the vices of his father. She blamed herself that the man she brought into the world was slowly but surely surrendering his immortal soul to the devil.

She stormed heaven for help. Day and night she prayed and wept and fasted, begging God to save her son and her family. Patiently she bore taunts and ridicule for his conversion.

But it seemed no use. Augustine went away to school

in Carthage where he joined the heretical Manichaeans and contracted an illicit union. While Augustine was at Carthage, his father died a good death within the Church.

Instead of despairing, St. Monica prayed the more. Augustine, spurning her entreaties, sailed to Italy, but he could not escape her prayers. There he met St. Ambrose who, after an almost incredible series of circumstances, finally received him into the Church. Augustine later became Bishop of Hippo and one of the greatest Fathers of the Western Church.

After Augustine's conversion, St. Monica considered her life's work finished. Shortly before her death she confided to him that there was nothing more she had wanted in life than the joy of seeing him a Christian.

"Monica," reads the second nocturn for her feast, "was really a mother in a twofold sense, because she brought her son both into the world and into heaven."

Such is the role of every true Catholic mother.

St. Nestor ☒

"Nestor" is used figuratively in English as a term of respect for an elderly man of great wisdom and courage. The word derives literally from the name of an aged hero of the Trojan War, as immortalized in Homeric legend. In the third century of the Christian era there was a saint called by the same name, a bishop whose see was located in Asia Minor, not too far from the city of the Iliad.

St. Nestor was accorded by his countrymen the same esteem given to the storied Hellenic elder. It even seems reasonable to assume that his name originated with the people themselves, in acknowledgment of his stature.

That stature was evidenced when Decian's imperial persecution was ordered enforced throughout the provinces. Having directed his flock to seek refuge in the mountains, St. Nestor stayed behind to face the enemy. His arrest was inevitable.

When St. Nestor was led into court, however, all present rose in deference to his reputation. For the same reason, the usual brutalities employed during trial inquisitions were dispensed with. And although threats of torture were voiced, the presiding judge could not bring himself to harm the saintly bishop.

So, in bonds, St. Nestor was delivered to the governor, who, like Pilate, eventually put personal ambition ahead of justice, and commanded that the aged prisoner be torn with iron hooks. When St. Nestor was promised surcease from the excruciating pain if only he would deny the Faith and sacrifice to the Roman gods, he cried out that he would not deny his Christ. For his courage he was eventually crucified.

The lesson to be learned in St. Nestor's life is that every bishop is bound, like the illustrious elder of Troy, to tower above his flock in wisdom and courage, and to be ready to face arrest and death at any moment for the Faith.

No one realizes this principle better than the prince of hell. From the beginnings of the Church even to today he has instructed those mortals in league with him that one of the surest means of breaking the faith of a people is by breaking their bishop. Witness, for example, the exquisite pains taken in the hope of destroying Cardinal Mindszenty or Cardinal Stepinac.

All of which should remind us of the position of a bishop and his need for our prayers.

St. Noel Chabanel ☖

It was the spring of the year 1643. From a harbor on
the west coast of France a young priest, Father Noel
Chabanel, set sail for Canada. As he landed in this
strange world three months later, he was admittedly
doubtful whether he would be able to withstand the
rigors of the missionary life for which he had volunteered. No one could have told him that he had the
makings of heroic sanctity, or that he would one day
be reckoned among the eight North American Martyrs.

A scholar at heart, Father Chabanel was recognized
in his home country as a teacher par excellence. In
temperament, he was quiet and unassuming; he loved
solitude, his books, a private room for reading and prayer.

Sent to work among the Algonquins, he found himself
unable to effect any conversions among them. Everything seemed to go wrong.

The vulgarities of the savages were repugnant to his
refined nature. No matter how he tried to overcome his
sensitivities, the cruelties of these Indians, their insipid
foods, the very smell of their bodies, drove him to
nausea. Often he would spend the night out in pillows
of wet snow rather than sleep within the filthy, over-
crowded cabins. And even after four years of effort, he
could not learn the simple Huron dialect.

Judging him a simpleton, the savages made great sport
of him, deliberately inventing fiendish schemes to torture or sicken him — like forcing him to eat human
flesh.

Thinking himself a complete failure, Father Chabanel
was tempted to return to France. For weeks he wavered.
And then he made a remarkable decision.

Kneeling before the Blessed Sacrament in a log chapel on Corpus Christi day, 1647, he took a vow of perpetual stability, promising he would never leave the Canadian missions of his own will. If it were God's will that he play the fool, the fool he would be.

He was murdered by an apostate Huron only two years later, years filled with self-abasement beyond description.

Total resignation to the divine will is the virtue that brought Father Chabanel to sanctity. Because God said No he broke into a thousand pieces his attachment to solitude and learning and went on to play the simpleton's role. His life is a stark example of the truth that it is not *what* we do that interests God, but *why* we do it. The only important role man ever performs in this life is the one God asks him to act. As Dante expressed it: "And in His will is our peace."

St. Oliver Plunket   ☩

There were two Oliver Plunkets in Irish history. One was Archbishop of Armagh, who was martyred in 1681 and whose canonization took place on October 12, 1975. The other Oliver died during the massacre of Fitzmaurice's ill-fated expedition at Smerwick Fort in Kerry; it is for him that the saint was named.

St. Oliver Plunket was a magnificent bishop. His witness calls to mind names such as Ignatius of Antioch, Cyprian of Carthage, and Patrick of Ireland, typical of the very best men with whom Christ's episcopate has been blessed over the centuries.

He left County Meagh for Rome at the age of sixteen to study for the priesthood. At that time, Ireland was in a state of political turmoil and anti-Catholic sentiment was strong. By 1654, the year of his ordination, the situation had so deteriorated that he was unable to return. For the next twelve years he taught theology at Propaganda College in Rome.

When the Metropolitan of Armagh died in exile in 1699, Father Plunket was named by Pope Clement IX to succeed. When he arrived in Ireland, by means of secret passage through England, he found himself to be the only bishop there, except for the aged Ordinary of Kilmore.

Partly because Blessed Oliver's heritage was noble, and partly because bigotry had somewhat waned, he was relatively free to perform regular episcopal functions. Thus, he convoked a much-needed synod, held two ordinations, and confirmed believers by the thousands. He began to enforce the decrees of Trent, put checks on Jansenistic trends, and helped the Jesuits build two schools. He even succeeded in reforming a group of desperate hill bandits.

With a renewed outbreak of anti-Catholicism, brought about by the spurious Titus Oates plot, Oliver was forced into hiding. In the cold and snow of the mountains south of Armagh, just before Christmas 1673, Plunket wrote: "Things are very bad here and, with another meeting of Parliament due on the 7th January next, they may get worse. I am in hiding . . ."

Pursued like an animal, he was finally seized for trial at Dublin, but when the Irish informers dared not accuse him in Ireland, the trial was moved to London. The rest of the story resembles that of most of the martyrs of that time: witnesses perjured themselves, various brutalities and indignities were employed, and the inevitable sentence of hanging, drawing, and quartering was pronounced. The blasphemous charge specified a "setting up" of a "false religion," and that "a greater crime cannot be committed against God than for a man to endeavor the propagation of that religion."

Plunket was a man of superior intellect and was very articulate. A modern-day successor, Armagh's Cardinal William Conway, once remarked that the saint was concerned about what we today call the media. Someone had drafted for him a final "speech from the scaffold," and smuggled it into his cell. But the archbishop did not like the draft; to him it was "too sharp" and abstract ("it goeth on generals"). So he rewrote the message in his own firm hand. (Remember Paul to the Galatians?) The manuscript is still extant. His version, he argued, "goeth on particulars which have more force of moving the sense and the ear." A few changes were pencilled by Father Corker and the message was smuggled out, to be released the morning of his execution.

Like St. Stephen's speech in the Acts of the Apostles, Plunket's message was both a rebuttal of the charges against him, and a plea for charity and tolerance. Stephen's speech has been the model for countless others throughout history.

St. Olga

St. Olga is often regarded as the first Russian to embrace the true Faith. Not so, however, for history attests to the presence of Christian bands along the shores of the Dnieper River from the very birth of the country of the Rous, or approximately a century before St. Olga's baptism in 955.

It is true, nonetheless, that this saintly woman was at least indirectly responsible for bringing Christ's Gospel to the newly established Slavic empire. St. Vladimir, her grandson, who is recognized as the Constantine of Russia, admitted that. For when he was debating whether or not he would enter the Church himself, it was the wonderful memory of St. Olga, he said, that finally occasioned his conversion.

Like most everyone born beyond the Carpathian ranges in the tenth century, St. Olga was reared as a pagan. Given in marriage to Igor, prince of Kiev, she was widowed when he was cruelly murdered. To avenge his death, she decreed (and this incident is indicative of her barbaric temperament prior to her conversion) that the assassins be scalded to death, and that their sympathizers be butchered by the hundreds.

Just what brought her to the acceptance of Christianity is unknown. Yet in 955 we find her in Constantinople humbly petitioning reception into the Church. And upon her return to Russia, she became a dynamic apostle of the Faith. She even arranged with the German emperor, Otto I, for Latin missionaries, but her plan was quickly and disastrously cut short, owing to deep-seated political distrust dividing East and West.

One of the most bitter crosses St. Olga had to bear was her son's refusal to become a Christian. Despite her prayers and continuous pleadings, the prince maintained one, almost inexplicable, excuse: "My men would laugh at me if I took up with a strange religion." This answer, according to the Russian chronicler Nestor, was for a long time typical of anti-Christian sentiment in the land of the Volga.

Typical, too, of an attitude common in Soviet Russia today, where many men still laugh at Christ.

Nevertheless, St. Olga must be praying for her people. For Soviet mockery is not so loud as it once was. There is much fear, we suspect, in Russian hearts today. And fear of God is the beginning of true wisdom.

St. Pambo ✠

It commonly happens in hagiography that the names of certain saints continue to remain popular long after their histories have been obscured by the ages.

Less frequently, and more oddly, the opposite occurs. The history, that is, of a particular saint remains substantially intact throughout epochs, but his name becomes almost completely obscured.

To exemplify this phenomenon, one has but to consider the fourth-century ascetic, St. Pambo. That he has not been remembered by Christendom is especially unfortunate, for he has much to offer.

During his early manhood, the deserts of Egypt became home for him. There, under the direction of the great monastic father, St. Anthony, he learned well the most practical lesson of his life: the fact of the relationship between sanctity and silence.

He finally selected discipline of the tongue as his own particular means for seeking perfection. For motivation he took for the text of his daily meditation the words of Psalm 38: "I will guard my ways, lest I sin with my tongue: I will put a bridle upon my mouth, while the wicked man stands before me."

Not that he failed to take advantage of all other means of sanctification utilized by the other monks of the desert. He too surrendered his frame to severe penances and fasts; he too prayed through most of the day; he too rounded out whatever free hours he had with hard manual labor.

But the secret of his sanctity really lay in his devotion to mortification of speech. So careful was he in his use of words that upon his deathbed he was able to say in all humility: "Since I came into the desert I do not remember that I ever said anything for which I had need to be sorry afterwards. . . ."

Such a statement is sobering in view of the fact that discipline of the tongue is requisite of every Christian.

What if every word we have ever uttered has been converted into another form of matter, from which it can one day be recaptured and played back for us to hear? The thought is not overly preposterous, is it, when one considers the principles of the conversion of matter into energy?

Besides, there is sure to be a playback, in the judgment each of us must face after death.

St. Patrick ☩

"Not deterred by cold, not possessed by hunger or thirst, sleeping on a bare stone, with a wet cloak around him, a rock for his pillow . . . enduring great trial." A capsule description, this, from Fiacc's "Hymn,"* of the life of one of history's most dynamic figures, St. Patrick of Ireland.

One dream kept revisiting him in the long years he spent studying for the priesthood. In it he could make out a courier bearing a message superscribed with the words "The Voice of the Irish." As he opened it, he would hear the plaintive cry of the people of Foclut begging him to "come and walk once more among us."

For six nightmarish years he had walked among them,

---

* From *St. Patrick* by Alice Curtayne in *Saints Are Not Sad* by F. J. Sheed, Copyright, 1949, Sheed and Ward, Inc., New York.

not by choice, but in wretched thralldom.

Kidnapped by corsairs while just a boy, he was carried overseas to the shores of Antrim and sold as chattel. Forced to live with the swine he herded on the slopes of Mount Slemish, he grew used to the mud and the bitter cold and the awful humiliations of a despised captive. But at the same time he began to learn the secret of prayerful resignation.

When, in response to a special inspiration, Patrick the slave finally took flight, he was already a saint in embryo. And already rooted in his soul was the burning desire to return one day to evangelize the poor pagans at whose hands he had suffered.

That wish was realized over twenty years later when Patrick the bishop leaped ashore at Strangford Lough in 432. The raging bonfire he set atop Slane that first Easter not only signaled the end of Druid paganism, but symbolized the brilliant light of the Faith that was to burn in the hearts of the Irish people from that moment down through the centuries, a fire that was to illumine not only Erin's isle, but all Western civilization as well.

Not that his task was an easy one. Constant prayer and severe self-mortifications were accompanied by brutal trials. Dangers from thieves and murderers, he related in his *Confessions*, occurred almost daily. There was also the treachery of his closest friend, followed by his most painful cross, his temporary deposition from office.

But 10 years after his landing, Ireland was already a stronghold of Catholicism with a hierarchy all its own, and countless parishes joining every part of it. Irish priests abounded, monasteries and convents dotted the isle, and new saints were being made.

If self-crucifixion is the sign of true love, no man ever loved the Irish more than St. Patrick. But St. Patrick was obviously one of God's closest friends.

St. Peter ☩

Bethsaida, a fishing village on the northeast corner of the Sea of Galilee, was the site of the birth of Simon Peter, the Prince of the Apostles. Originally a disciple of St. John the Baptist, he immediately accepted Christ as the Lamb of God once the Precursor had pointed out his cousin as the Messias. With his brother Andrew (who also became one of the Twelve), he followed the Savior for many months, until consideration of his family's support forced him to return to his fishing trade on the lake of his youth.

There he received his vocation to the apostolate. His beloved Master had just finished speaking to the multitudes assembled on the shore. It was Simon's boat Christ used for a pulpit — almost as if to prophesy how His voice soon would be heard only from Peter's barque. Now, when the people had gone home, Christ asked Simon to go fishing once again.

Peter hesitated for a moment (the previous night had yielded only empty nets), then set forth into the deep. The miraculous draft of fishes followed. And after that, Christ's call.

The rest of the Apostle's life is well known: how he blurted forth his love for Christ only to betray it on Holy Thursday night; how he promised never to desert his Master, yet abandoned Him at Gethsemane and on Golgotha. Nevertheless, Simon was the one whom Christ called to be His first pontiff, His "bridge-builder" between heaven and earth: ". . . Thou art Peter, and upon this rock I will build my Church . . . I will give thee the keys of the kingdom of heaven . . . Feed my sheep. . . ."

After Pentecost, Peter governed the See of Antioch, then founded the capital of Christendom at Rome. There he was crucified, head downward, about A.D. 67. His tomb, recently rediscovered, lies directly beneath the dome of the magnificent basilica that bears his name.

In St. Peter we see clearly the key to holiness, namely, a pure and profound love for Christ. So intensely did the first Apostle love his Lord that even the awful guilt of his triple denial was washed from his soul. Not only that, but he was selected by the Savior for a role no man even dared dream of: Peter, the impetuous blunderer, was asked to be Christ's very Vicar!

St. Pius X ☩

In 1903 there succeeded to the Chair of Peter, by a seemingly accidental turn of events, a relatively unknown prelate, possessed of practically no experience at all in pontifical functions or ecclesiastical diplomacy. Eleven years later he died. Yet in that brief span he had already been recognized as one of the Church's most illustrious and holy Supreme Pontiffs. In 1954 he became the first pope to be canonized since 1672. His name, of course, is Pope St. Pius X.

For seventeen long years he remained a simple curate. Then, suddenly, he found himself appointed bishop of Mantua, a poor, spiritually bankrupt see. Suddenly again, eight years later, he became archbishop of Venice, his native land.

The biggest surprise of all came in 1903. After seven ballots (and much sensation following the Austrian em-

peror's formal "veto" of one of the leading candidates),
Giuseppe Sarto of Riese was elected Pope Pius X.

At once he instituted a vigorous program of practical
reform. He redesigned the educational system of Catholic colleges and seminaries, regulated the teaching of
Christian doctrine, established a commission for the
textual study of the Latin Vulgate. The spadework for
the codification of canon law and the reorganization of
the Roman congregations were both of his doing. For
these last two accomplishments especially, the London
Times editorialized that he would go down in history
as the great legislator of modern times.

In 1905 he issued his immortal decree on the Blessed
Eucharist, urging the faithful to receive the Blessed
Sacrament as often as possible, and permitting children
to make their First Communion upon attaining the use
of reason.

As a crusader he dealt the deathblow to the heresy of
Modernism, an adaptation of Kantian subjectivism to
dogma. And he freed the French hierarchy from the
chains of the state.

Despite the demands and trials of his papacy, his
holiness of life was magnified day by day. To evidence
it to the world, God worked miraculous cures through
him.

He died, as poor as he had been born, in 1914, the
same day the German armies marched into Brussels.

The key to Pope St. Pius X's sanctity was the motto
he took for his pontificate: "To restore all things in
Christ."

In following this motto perfectly, any one of us could
become a saint. For Christ alone, in His own words, is
"the way, the truth, and the life."

St. Quentin ☦

St. Quentin's Day is hardly even adverted to in the modern world; few Catholics, if any, ever invoke the saint.

His existence is attested to by the fact, for instance, that St. Gregory, the famed bishop of sixth-century Tours, alludes in one of his writings to an early French church named for the saint. (There is a magnificent basilica standing to his honor in France today.) And St. Gregory's remarks indicate that St. Quentin was a martyr.

The Irish missionaries apparently had special devotion for St. Quentin too. Thus it is recorded that toward the close of the seventh century St. Foillan (one of the best known of the lesser missionary monks) celebrated a special Mass on the eve of St. Quentin's Day before setting out on a difficult apostolic assignment.

There are practically no historic details of the saint's life, however. According to his legend (which was evidently known of by St. Bede, the chronicler of English beginnings), St. Quentin was a Roman who had undertaken the evangelization of the territory encompassing Amiens. Arrested and tortured for the Faith by the prefect Rictiovarus, he was finally put to death at August Veromanduorum, the site of the present Saint-Quentin. His body was then cast into the Somme, but was recovered by the faithful and buried near the town.

Of what advantage is it for us to pause for any length of time to recall so minor a saint?

There are several good reasons. First, as St. Thomas points out, it is only fitting that all those who have attained God's special friendship should be revered —

not only the major saints who are universally honored.

Second, because variety in invoking the saints is spiritually profitable; it helps to stimulate interest in heavenly things, increase devotion, dispel apathy.

And finally, but principally, because God in His wisdom wanted St. Quentin to be known and venerated — though for what specific reason, as yet we know not. But is it so important that we do know?

St. René Goupil ✠

The first of the North American Martyrs to die was René Goupil. A physician by profession, he gave up a successful practice in France to offer himself as a *donne* (i.e., a lay assistant committed by private vows) for the Indian missions of the New World. As a youth he had, in fact, entered the Jesuit novitiate at Paris, but left because of sickness.

In 1642, Goupil set out for the Huron territory with Father Isaac Jogues. The story of how their party was ambushed by a band of Mohawks is well known from the many accounts of Jogues' own life. With the heroic priest, Goupil was beaten, transported to camp (during the awful journey he was received as a professed member of the Society of Jesus by Jogues), made to run the gauntlet, tortured atop a platform, sent through the gauntlet and publicly subjected to irons and fire again, horribly mutilated, and finally enslaved.

Goupil's sufferings were cut short suddenly when a young brave surprised him from behind, driving a tomahawk deep into his brain. As Jogues knelt down to impart final absolution, a blood-crazed mob snatched up the body for a wild orgy. "Thus, on the 29th of September," wrote Jogues in his diary, "this angel of innocence and martyr of Jesus Christ was immolated in his thirty-fifth year for Him who had given His life for ransom."

Later Father Jogues found the desecrated corpse of his comrade and buried it beneath a monument of stones, evidently in the same ravine that still cuts through the Shrine of the North American Martyrs near Albany, New York. But it was stolen again by the Mohawks and cast as so much refuse in the woods. When Jogues finally recovered it, he buried what was left with a prayer for the future of this country.

René Goupil was a layman until the beginning of his last agony. Can we not see in his martyrdom a prophecy that the American layman is destined to play one of the most significant roles ever in the evangelization of a nation? Has not part of this prophecy already been fulfilled?

St. Rita of Cascia ☗

How she ever had it in her heart to forgive her husband the constant pain he kept causing her, the townspeople simply could not fathom. Not one of them had a good word for him; they knew that he was dissolute, that he treated her shamefully, that he had actually betrayed his marital vows many times. Yet, despite their protestations, St. Rita of Cascia was determined to stay with the man she married through eighteen years of torture until (as it happened just before his sudden death) she could lead him to repentance and the state of grace.

Her husband's profligate life was not the only cross this woman was asked to carry. Her two sons, despite her prayers and admonitions, grew to imitate their father's perverse ways.

Following his brutal murder (probably the result of a vendetta), the boys vowed revenge. They would have carried through with their criminal scheme, had not St. Rita asked God — and here we find St. Rita in the most tragic circumstances in which a mother can find herself — to take their lives, rather than permit them to commit their planned crime.

God answered her prayer. Both sons fell seriously ill, and, to her extreme sorrow, soon died in her arms; but, to her great joy, in the state of grace.

A lonely widow now, she applied for admission to a community of nuns at Cascia near her home town of Roccaporena, in the Apennines. Ironically, it was the same convent she had wanted to enter as a child.

The convent was reluctant to accept her now, however. She was a widow, and there was the added problem of her advanced age. Yet, after much persistence, St. Rita was finally received in 1413.

For the next 44 years she lived a life of perfection, not only by keeping the difficult rule, but by assuming extraordinary fasts and penances — all for the conversion of sinners. In 1441 she received the sacred stigmata, in the form of an open wound on her forehead. The scar became so ugly and festered that she was finally forbidden to mix socially with the other nuns.

An excruciating, wasting disease slowly reduced her body to lifelessness. Death occurred in 1447.

Wives who are mocked or maltreated by their husbands have in St. Rita a patroness who can buoy up their hearts in the midst of the deepest of sorrows. In her they have a model who, under the most tragic terms possible, actually fulfilled the solemn vow to love one's partner "for worse."

St. Servulus ☒

St. Servulus is doubtless a total stranger to the average Christian today. Not a church hereabouts bears his name — not even a shrine. And he is hardly ever mentioned in the standard *Lives of the Saints*, save in some of the more exhaustive compilations.

He was widely known as a saint during his very lifetime, however, and during the generations directly following. That would take us back to the latter part of the sixth century, during the pontificate of St. Gregory the Great. The pope apparently knew Servulus closely, for he cites this now obscure saint as a model of virtue in some of his celebrated sermons.

A deformed paralytic, Servulus used to spend his days begging for alms before the Church of St. Clement, on the Caelian Hill in the Eternal City. Each morning he was carried there by his mother and brother, propped up against the gate wall, then left alone to the bustling crowds and to God.

From the crowds he received enough for food, medicine, and a few fragments of Sacred Scripture and other spiritual writings. If anything remained, he gave it to the poor, or to other unfortunates like himself.

From God he received gifts far more precious. During the long hours he lay in the heat or cold, or dust or rain, he gradually became aware that God was talking to him as a Friend to a friend. And in his forced solitude he learned how to listen to God speaking.

Soon he became so docile to the mysterious workings of divine grace that his heart began to thrill with the consciousness that he was selected from all eternity to be a victim of reparation for sin — which is, after all, the divine plan for all those born into this world so deformed or maimed.

Thus his soul grew stronger in resignation, peace, and grace until, in the year 590, he passed, like the beggar Lazarus of St. Luke's parable, to his eternal reward. He was buried in St. Clement's Church.

In one of his panegyrics, Pope St. Gregory cites Servulus as a person whose example censures those who, while gifted with wealth and a measure of worldly joy, fail to share their riches with others less fortunate, and who refuse to suffer the least cross which comes their way.

A good thought, this. Perhaps it can inspire us to works of true charity this year, particularly toward the countless unfortunates of our own community, who, like Servulus, have been selected by God as victims, in the expectation that we will honor them as such, and help them fulfill their role — to our spiritual advantage as well as theirs.

St. Simeon Stylites ☩

St. Simeon Stylites the Younger is not the same person as the St. Simeon Stylites. The former lived a century later, and is not so well known as the latter. But like all the so-called "pillar saints," he is among the least understood saints of history.

He was not just a flagpole sitter with a motive. That he did spend most of his days atop a column (the Greek word is *stulos*) is attested by numerous eyewitnesses of unquestionable veracity. But his column certainly had no relationship whatever to a flagpole. Rather, it was some kind of a supported elevation — a platform on stilts, no doubt. This much is clear from the fact that he was able to celebrate Mass and distribute Communion on it.

As a boy, Simeon made his way to the mountain districts outside Antioch, in order to join the disciples of the great mystic, John the Stylite. But the pupil soon became more famed than his master. To escape the pilgrims who began to seek him out, he eventually took refuge on an isolated hill, where he remained in almost continual prayer for the next ten years.

In 547 he moved his platform to a new site, around which he built a monastery. Here he remained for almost half a century, achieving international renown not only as one of the most venerable men of his time, but also as one of the most eccentric. Thus, in the tradition of the Stylites, he would remain standing, all day and most of the night, in all kinds of weather; subject himself to painful disciplines; prophesy; and so on. His holiness was confirmed by God in that he was given the power to work miracles and effect cures.

Because of his strange ways, St. Simeon — like all the other Stylites — has been made the target of considerable ridicule by non-Christians. This is really somewhat ironic, for the "pillar saints" are not at all difficult to comprehend.

It is only necessary to remember that the pillars of the "pillar saints" had no essential connection at all with their sanctity. St. Simeon the Younger and the other Stylites became saints for one reason only; they loved God with an extraordinary love.

St. Simon Stock ✠

It was to St. Simon Stock that our Blessed Lady announced the promise of the Brown Scapular. Appearing with the scapular in her hands, she said: *"This will be a privilege to you and to all Carmelites; whosoever dies wearing this shall not suffer eternal fires."*

This apparition, attested to by solid and weighty evidence, took place in 1251. Four years earlier Simon Stock had been elected superior general of the Carmelite Order.

In those four brief years, the growth of the Order had been phenomenal. Many new houses were being established in various countries throughout Europe; numerous candidates were presenting themselves for admission.

The rapid progress of the Carmelites in Europe was all the more extraordinary because they had originated not on the continent, but in the East. Their primitive foundations, moreover, were eremitical rather than monastic; their mode of life more contemplative than active. Simon himself had probably joined the Order as a hermit in the Holy Land, but returned to England with most other religious there when the Saracens conquered the land.

It was precisely when the Order was at the crossroads of its history — when it was evolving in rule and in outlook — that St. Simon was favored with his vision. From that moment on, the fate of the Carmelites was sealed as one of the world's greatest religious organizations. And ever since, of course, the very term "Carmelite" has been synonymous with Marian devotion.

St. Simon died in 1265, and was buried near Bordeaux.

In 1951 his relics were transferred from that city to the recently restored Carmelite house at Aylesford in Kent.

What lesson is paramount in the life of St. Simon Stock? The very fact that Mary chose to appear to him indicates that there must have been many. But it is principally in the message she asked him to promulgate that we find most food for meditation. That message can be summed up in this wise: Anyone who wears the scapular with sincerity and devotion as the insignia of Mary, who takes us to her Son, can rely with confidence on the Scapular Promise.

Which is certainly one of the most important messages yet delivered to the world by a saint.

St. Stephen, Protomartyr ☒

The first martyr to die for the Faith was neither an Apostle nor one of the seventy disciples of our Lord. He was evidently a Jew, however; though his name — Stephanos is a Greek expression meaning "crown" — indicates that he might have been a member of the Diaspora, the Hellenists who made their homes beyond Palestine. Christian tradition has long referred to him as St. Stephen the Protomartyr, and from the fourth century has observed his feast on December 26.

Everything we know about his history is found in St. Luke's Acts of the Apostles. He appears there as one of the first deacons ordained by the Twelve to assist them in the lesser works of the ministry.

"Now Stephen, full of grace and power," the Acts read, "was working great wonders and signs among the people. But there arose some from the synagogue which is called that of the Freedmen, and of the Cyrenians and of the Alexandrians and of those from Cilicia and the province of Asia, disputing with Stephen. And they were not able to withstand the wisdom and the Spirit who spoke. Then they bribed men to say they had heard him speaking blasphemous words against Moses and against God" (Verse 6, 8–11).

So Stephen was arrested and brought before the Sanhedrin. A twofold indictment was pronounced against him: he had declared that the temple would be destroyed, and that the Mosaic Covenant had been superseded by the New Testament, recently sealed in the Blood of the Son of God Incarnate, Christ Jesus.

After his accusers had withdrawn, Stephen was given leave to speak. His address, recorded at length by St. Luke, is a remarkable exposition of how Scripture was fulfilled in Christ. At the close he severely censured his official persecutors as a "stiff-necked" race. Thereupon, he saw the heavens open, and Christ standing at the right hand of the Father.

Enraged, the Jews dragged St. Stephen outside the city walls to stone him. And as he sank in agony beneath the raining tower of rocks, he was heard praying aloud for his murderers.

Which is, perhaps, one of the chief reasons why St. Stephen's feast is so proximate to Christmas. For did not Christ become Man (to die for man) for love of man? But is not every man a sinner? And is not every sinner God's enemy?

St. Stephen's love for his enemies, as evidenced in his martyrdom, partakes of the love of Christ for sinners — a love so evident during Christmastide.

St. Theodore ✠

The martyrdom of St. Theodore happened over fifteen centuries ago, yet it reads like a modern story of religious persecution behind the Iron Curtain.

Then, the forces of evil were marshaled by the impious despot, Julian the Apostate. Filled with an intense hatred for Christianity and the "despicable Galileans" who professed it, he was determined to reduce the name of Christ to a mere symbol.

Clever, he realized that open persecution was not feasible: since Constantine's conversion and the Edict of Milan, Christianity had become an integral part of the empire.

He began by usurping all Church property. Next, he set up a new state religion, complete with a hierarchy. From the confiscated estates he paid his clergy well.

The intimidation of Catholic priests followed. For those who refused to apostatize, there was torture; and after torture, either exile or death.

The final phase consisted in systematic discrimination against the faithful. Overnight, Christians were ejected from all responsible positions, and from the schools and universities.

Particularly resistant to Julian's diabolical campaign was the Catholic center of Antioch, in the East. There the faithful, led by the influential and saintly priest, Theodore, remained unshaken in their loyalty to Christ. Their churches closed, they continued to assemble secretly for Mass and prayer. It was obvious to the emperor that Theodore must be silenced. For that purpose he appointed his own uncle, Julian the Prefect.

With a new reign of terror, the prefect profaned all

discovered places of worship, and soon forced most of the clergy into exile. Still, Theodore remained to preach and to minister to his flock, but his capture was inevitable.

As an example to the faithful he was savagely tortured, but he would not break. "After the torment of the rack and many other severe tortures, including the burning of his sides, with torches," reads the *Marytrology*, "he still persisted in the confession of Christ. . . ." He died in 362, his martyrdom completed with the sword.

Like St. Theodore, countless priests today have stood up before the onslaught of godless tyranny. Like him, too, they have been mangled, and have died. And like him, little is known of their complete history, save that they did die for Christ's Kingdom, and that their deaths will surely avail for the ultimate conquest of Christ over Satan. As the lawyer Tertullian warned the Roman Empire years before Julian's time: "The blood of martyrs is the seed of the Church."

There is a sequel. The year after St. Theodore's death, Julian the Apostate was violently slain by the Persian cavalry. The story spread among the people that he cried to heaven as he died: "Galilean, thou hast conquered!"

St. Thomas Aquinas   ☩

How is it possible to epitomize the life and accomplishments of St. Thomas Aquinas? Yet if a simple profile has to be drawn, it must emphasize, in clear bold lines, the supreme truth that his matchless genius — that breathtaking brilliance before which the world still stands and will ever stand in awe — was surely shadowed by his angelic holiness.

As a young student in Naples, he used to steal away from the university campus to the nearby Dominican church, there to spend long hours in quiet, profound contemplation of the Blessed Sacrament. His union with our divine Lord grew closer with the years, and was sealed in an extraordinary manner with his ordination to the priesthood. While pronouncing the sacred words of Consecration at Mass, records one of his biographers, he would become totally absorbed in the mystery being enacted.

Once during the years in which he was composing the *Summa Theologica* — the peerless synthesis of Christian theology — our blessed Lord spoke to him as he knelt in ecstasy before the crucifix: "Thou hast written well of me, Thomas; what reward wouldst thou have?" With the spontaneity characteristic of St. Peter the Apostle, he immediately replied: "Nothing but Thyself, O Lord."

So pleasing to God was this response, that the humble Dominican began to experience mystical lights no mortal could dare dream. His union with the Divine became so intense and overpowering that he finally had to put aside the *Summa*, leaving it unfinished. He stopped writing on the feast of St. Nicholas in 1273. During Mass on that day he received a revelation so ineffable that he was compelled to explain: "All that I have written appears to be as so much straw after the things that have been revealed to me."

As he lay dying in a Cistercian abbey in 1274 (he had fallen ill on his way to the Council of Lyons, to which he had been invited by Pope Gregory X), he stated once more the sole motivation underlying his superhuman intellectual conquests, his every earthly deed or thought. Receiving the Bread of Heaven for the final time, he prayed in words not even Dante could better: "I am receiving Thee, Price of my soul's redemption: all my studies, my vigils and my labors have been for love of thee. . . ."

The paramount lessons from the life of St. Thomas? That man's intellect, howsoever brilliant, was created by God from nothing for the sole purpose of glorifying God. And that, besides God, everything else is straw.

St. Vincent de Paul   ✠

Any list of history's most influential figures would be incomplete without mention of the amazing seventeenth-century organizer and innovator, St. Vincent de Paul.

He stands at the beginnings of almost all modern Christian humanitarianism. He laid the foundations for our present hospital system and the nursing profession. He was the first in his land to build suitable foundling homes and orphanages. He organized social agencies to aid the poor, the imprisoned, the galley slaves. He pioneered the establishment of institutions for the aged, the incurably diseased, the mentally ill.

From a spiritual view, his accomplishments were no less phenomenal, nor less revolutionary. He founded the Congregation of the Mission, a group of secular priests (popularly known as the Vincentians) who also take religious vows. From his inspiration, sprang the now famed Daughters of Charity, Sisters whose convent, in his own words, was to be "the sickroom" . . . their cloister, "the streets of the city." Through this community, he set the course for all the other semicloistered Sisterhoods since founded to work among men in the professions, such as teaching, nursing, social work.

He had a hand, too, in drawing the plans for today's seminary program, in the initial development of the lay retreat movement; and so on, almost *ad infinitum*.

How one person could ever have accomplished so much seems unfathomably mysterious at first. It becomes more enigmatic when one considers the harsh circumstances of the saint's life.

Born into poverty in Gascony, he was sent to school only because he had no aptitude for farming. Newly ordained after much personal hardship, he was seized by pirates and carried off to Tunis, where he was sold into slavery. Face to face with the most profound human misery now, he began to realize the virtue of helping others for the love of Christ.

So, not long after his escape, he began blueprinting his life's apostolate of charity. Once begun, that apostolate did not cease until his death at the age of eighty, in 1660.

One fact of St. Vincent's life seems most striking; namely, the sheer universality of his undertakings. He did not limit his apostolate to *just* the poor, or to *just* the orphans, or to *just* the sick. Instead he tried everything for everyone, all for the sake of his Savior.

How did he do it? The answer must be contained in St. Paul's words, words upon which we would do well often to reflect: "I can do all things in him who strengthens me."

St. Zita

To the socially prominent guests invited to the great manor of thirteenth-century Lucca's wealthy Fatinelli family, St. Zita was no more than another servant girl. They may have noticed her kindness in carrying out their demands or her unusual patience. But doubtless few realized that the quiet little girl who worked in the kitchens and served at table was especially close to the heart of God.

She was born and raised on a poor dirt farm in the Tuscan village of Monte Sagrati, where her parents eked out an existence from the soil. As a child she knew hunger and privation. Before she entered her teens, she was already contributing to the family support by peddling vegetables and fruits to the townspeople of nearby Lucca. It was there that she met the influential Fatinelli family, whose service she entered at 18.

Her work as a maid (and later as housekeeper) she was determined to use as her personal ladder to holiness.

Every moment of drudgery she consecrated to God: the long hours spent in the kitchens, preparing foods and washing dishes; in the great serving halls, catering to guests; in the parlors and corridors, dusting costly cabinets and sweeping rugs; in the laundries, cleaning the sumptuous clothes of the rich.

For spiritual strength, she sacrificed an hour of sleep to attend Mass every morning. Her food she often gave to the poor, herself fasting or living on scraps.

As one might suspect, her sanctity was not appreciated at first. Her employers treated her harshly and unfairly; Some fellow servants conspired against her. Ultimately, however, all bowed before the greatness of the quiet little maid.

Miracles began to happen at the manor. Loaves of bread she had forgotten to prepare were ready for the oven upon her return from church. Food she had given away was suddenly replenished beyond human explanation.

During her later days, her employers tried to lighten her domestic tasks, but she would have little of such an arrangement. To take away her duties as a servant would be to remove the very keystone of her sanctification.

She died in 1278, and is venerated today as the patroness of maids and domestic help.

The life of St. Zita is a vivid reminder that holiness is often found where the world least suspects it; in the kitchen, for example. It is a lesson, too, that God in His tremendous love is no respecter of the outer trappings of men, nor of the mansions wherein they dwell. He looks only into their hearts.

Appendix:
Saints without the "St."

VENERABLE KATERI TEKAKWITHA

Kateri Tekakwitha, the seventeenth-century Indian maiden whose cause for beatification is under study, was probably born at the fortressed Mohawk village of Ossernenon, which is now the National Shrine of the American Martyrs at Auriesville (just off New York Thruway Exits 27 and 28). It is possible that she was born a few miles away from the shrine on the north shore of the Mohawk river. Perhaps her family moved after a smallpox epidemic in 1661, for there is evidence to the effect that she spent her early years as a Christian at Gandahouhague (i.e. "the rapids"), which has been identified with an area bordering present-day Fonda.

The confusion is understandable, especially in view of the facts that (1) Iroquois villages were constantly being moved, some of them as frequently as every ten years; and (2) a transported village often kept the same name it previously had, even if it embraced two or more sections.

The date of her birth is usually given as 1656, ten years after the intrepid St. Isaac Jogues underwent martyrdom at Ossernenon. Her father was an Iroquois pagan; her mother, an Algonquin convert. Both died while Kateri (i.e., Catherine) was still very young. She became the ward of an uncle who was a village chieftain.

She was called "Tekakwitha" (the Iroquois *Tegahkouita*) from her early childhood. According to the usual explanation, the word means "she who sets things in order." (I once checked with a Church historian who looked up the word in an Iroquois lexicon, where it was given as a form of *Tekkwitha*, and defined as "she approaches." He also told me that one commentator believes the name really signifies "one who advances, moving things before her," and that another has interpreted this with reference to the partial blindness she suffered as a result of smallpox; i.e. like one who moves cautiously, feeling for objects to avoid stumbling.)

Kateri's blindness actually promoted her first steps to holiness. Because she had to remain in the dark corners of the cabin, since her eyes were unable to tolerate bright light, she could more easily protect her soul from being tainted by the indecencies, obscenities and sadistic torture-orgies which occurred in her Mohawk village.

The history of Kateri's conversion and baptism by the holy Father James de Lamberville has been told many times; so, too, that of the humiliations, slanders and physical sufferings she had to endure as a Christian and of her eventual flight (with her uncle in close pursuit) to La Prairie de la Magdeleine in 1667. However, the story of her days at the Canadian mission is not detailed in many of the popular accounts.

Evidently her personal road to perfection was extreme self-mortification for the love of God. At first the penances she assumed were difficult enough — mixing earth with her food, for instance, though so discreetly that it was hardly noted by others. But with the news that the converts at La Prairie were marked for torture and death by the Iroquois cantons, she led the way in preparing for possible martyrdom by self-disciplines so excessive that, declares her eighteenth-century chronicler, "the missionaries would never have permitted them had they been fully informed in regard to them."

After a visit to Montreal, the sight of a community of nursing sisters fired her with new zeal to consecrate herself to God by a vow of chastity. After much pleading she was given permission to do so, and thus became the first of her nation to be numbered as a Spouse of Christ.

The story of her final days is especially moving. Severely weakened by her penances, she nonetheless sought out every opportunity to multiply and intensify them. She would walk barefoot in the snow, or would cover her simple bed with live thorns. The only hours she was free from pain were those she used to spend before the Blessed Sacrament where, we are told, she would remain prostrate till her entire frame was numbed by the cold.

As death neared she remained alone on a pallet, with only a dish of Indian corn and some water at her side. On Wednesday of Holy Week in the year 1680, the Lily of the Mohawks passed from this world to the next, hand-in-hand, no doubt, with the Queen of Virgins — to a land where the light no longer pained her eyes but healed them forever.

Real vision is spiritual sight.

BISHOP FREDERIC BARAGA

Bishop Frederic Baraga, whose beatification the bishops of the United States formally encouraged in the 1972 meeting, was recognized by many as a saint early in his priestly career. He was a Slovenian immigrant who became the apostle of the Indians in what is now upper Michigan and northern Wisconsin, and was the first Shepherd of the Diocese of Marquette.

Four specific aspects of Bishop Baraga's life point to his heroic witness to the Faith. First, he was preeminently a man of prayer. According to Chrysostom Verwyst, one of his American biographers, Baraga spent two to three hours every morning in prayer. Even when he travelled long distances through the cold, snow-filled woods, he was always up before dawn to meditate and begin his Office. Often he would finish his prayers at nigh, by the light of a campfire, even though he was numb with cold. While he was at LaPoint he initiated the practice of rising at 3 A.M. in the summer, and 4 A.M. in winter, to ensure himself enough prayer time before the rush of each day's events.

Second, Baraga was a preacher *par excellence*. Typical passages from his diary cite five sermons a day. He taught catechism several times a week whenever he wasn't visiting his mission outposts. And in his spare time he worked on his various devotional manuals, catechisms, and "gospel-books." For the Chippewa mission at L'Anse, for example he translated parts of the Bible, the common Catholic prayers and hymns, and had these works (together with a Chippewa grammar) published at his own expense.

Finally, Bishop Barage was a thoroughly committed and contagiously enthusiastic cultic leader. To celebrate Mass was for him the summit of priestly and personal fulfillment. He prepared and conducted the liturgy with utmost care, desirous that even the least appointment or ceremony would serve to impress all who had assembled with a clear appreciation of the majestic holiness of the Eucharistic Sacrifice.

He heard confessions long hours at a time; his diary simply refers to "many" confessions heard day after day. He baptized and conferred the Sacrament of Confirmation with an obvious love of what he was doing. As for the Sacrament of the Sick, one eyewitness once recalled that he responded to the sick calls in wintertime in showshoes.

Finally, Baraga's priestly zeal was phenomenal. "We see him . . . building churches, equipping little schools, establishing Christian colonies, teaching the things of God and man," wrote Cardinal Amleto G. Cicognani in *Sanctity in America*. He went on and on, through the endless woods on snowshoes or else on dogsled, over the choppy waters of the lakes in birch-bark canoes. And his only purpose was to announce the living Lord Jesus.

As Baraga himself noted in his diary: "The snow was very deep and the temperature bitterly cold, but the salvation of a single immortal soul is worth more than all the millions of the world."

"His life was so perfect," wrote a convert who knew him, "and he explained the teaching of the Church with a simplicity so intelligent and so courageous that everyone honored him as a Catholic. He would explain our devotion to the Mother of God with the utmost clearness . . . or quote our great spiritual writers in a way to account best for the faith he bore. When I was young I used to hear Protestants speak with reverence of two Catholics — the great Fenelon and the humble Toussaint. . ."

Just before he passed to his eternal reward, Toussaint said, "God is with me."

Of course. And may God grant a return of Toussaint's spirit in New York City and the nation today.

PIERRE TOUSSAINT

Men and women, lay and religious, black and white mourned the passing of this great man.

An eyewitness gave this description of the funeral of one of New York City's most remarkable Christians, the black hairdresser Pierre Toussaint, who died on 30 June 1853, in his 87th year. The funeral took place in old St. Peter's on Barclay St.; the burial in old St. Patrick's Churchyard, at a site now designated by a plaque blessed by Cardinal Francis Spellman of New York in 1951.

Toussaint arrived in Manhattan in 1787. Born in servitude, he had accompanied his masters, the Berards, when they fled Haiti's political strife, which was generated in part by the French Revolution. As a result of chance conversation, Madame Berard arranged for Toussaint to learn the hairdresser's art — a circumstance that changed both his life and the lives of countless New Yorkers.

For one thing, when his master died and his investments failed, Toussaint became the family's breadwinner, literally supporting Madame Berard and the household. As a hairdresser he was an immediate success; in fact, he quickly became a prominent personage, whose clientele included some of Gotham's socially elite.

But Toussaint was a hairdresser with saintly motives. Christian kindness radiated from him; he was a friend to the poor, the orphaned, the lonely, the alienated. He lived the Sermon on the Mount; one of his friends one noted that "his pity for the suffering seemed to partake of the character of the Saviour's tenderness at the tomb of Lazarus." He personally nursed the dying, brought food to the hungry, educated scores of black youths, paid for the schooling of seminarians, supported priests. And his absolute resignation to the divine will was evidenced in his humble acceptance of his adopted daughter's death.

People sought out his gracious benediction; "more than one of his acquaintances grew to refer to him as 'my own St. Pierre.'" One woman once added that "nobody has a better saint."

The scope of Toussaint's charitable endeavors came to full light when the executors of his will went through his papers. They found a crucifix with an appended note, "To Toussaint from the grateful priest"; documents of manumission testifying to his part in redeeming slaves prior to the New York emancipation Act of July, 1800; varied letters of appreciation from priests whom he had aided financially while they were in the seminary; references to a mission he had funded in Haiti; notes concerning his aid to New York's orphaned, to

Bishop Benedict J. Fenwick of Boston, and to various institutions.

Acknowledgments

We should like to express our gratitude to the publishers of the revised complete edition of *Butler's Lives of the Saints* (New York: P. J. Kenedy, 1956) for their permission to use quotations attributed to the saints according to the versions given in *Butler's Lives*. And we would also like to thank both the publishers of the Confraternity New Testament (Confraternity of Christian Doctrine, 1941) and the publishers of the English version of the *Roman Martyrology* (The Newman Press, *The Roman Martyrology*, 1946) for permission to quote from their works. All the New Testament scriptural texts are from the Confraternity version.

Bibliography

Butler's Lives of the Saints, Complete Edition, edited, revised, and supplemented by Herbert Thurston, S.J., and Donald Attwater (New York: P. J. Kenedy and Sons, 1956).

The Catholic Encyclopedia, 15 vols. (New York: Robert Appleton Company, 1907).

The Roman Martyrology, translated by Rev. Joseph B. Collins (Westminster, Md.: The Newman Bookshop, 1946).

A History of the Catholic Church, Fernand Mourret, S.S., translated by Rev. Newton Thompson, S.T.D., 7 vols. (St. Louis: B. Herder Book Co., 1931).

A History of the Catholic Church, Dom Charles Poulet, 2 vols., from the Fourth French Edition by Sidney A. Raemers (St. Louis: B. Herder Book Co., 1940).

The Lives of the Saints, Omer Englebert, translated by Christopher and Anne Freemantle (New York: David McKay Company, Inc., 1951).

The Life of Christ, Giuseppe Ricciotti, translated by Alba I. Zizzamia (Milwaukee: The Bruce Publishing Company, 1947).

The Jesuit Relations and Allied Documents, Reuben Gold Thwaites, "Travel and Explorations of the Jesuit Missionaries in New France" (Cleveland: The Burrows Brothers Company, 1896–1901).

The American Martyrs, John A. O'Brien (New York: Appleton-Century-Crofts, Inc., 1953).

Handbook of Christian Feasts and Customs, Francis X. Weiser, S.J. (New York: Harcourt, Brace and Company, 1952).

Saints Are Not Sad, assembled by F. J. Sheed (New York: Sheed and Ward, 1949).

Alice in Wonderland, Lewis Carroll (New York: The Modern Library, Random House).

The Poems and Plays of Robert Browning (New York: The Modern Library, Random House).

Breviarium Romanum (New York: Benziger Brothers, 1949).

169

Other Resource Materials

Books

FRIENDS AREN'T KEPT WAITING, by Father Francis LeBuffe, S.J., Updated by Catharine Hughes. Modern reflections of spirituality drawn from the lives of different people, related to a Scriptural text and concluding with an appropriate prayer.

—**$1.75,** Paper

ELIZABETH ANN SETON — Mother, Teacher, Saint for Our Time, by Jane F. Hindman. Every American will find inspiration in this biography of the indomitable woman who flaunted convention to follow her conscience. Her simply told story dramatizes that sanctity is achievable by any Christian willing to live the faith fully and without reservation.

—**$1.50,** Paper

THE GOSPEL OF THE HOLY SPIRIT by Alfred P. McBride, O. Praem. A popular study edition of the Acts of the Apostles which dramatizes the permeating presence of the Holy Spirit in the primitive Church of Peter and Paul. Father McBride's commentary underlines the striking parallel—of disagreements, tensions, and dissatisfaction—of those early days with the turmoil following Vatican II.

—**$1.50,** Paper (Resource Guide, 75¢)

GENESIS REGAINED by F. J. Sheed. The highly respected publisher-author-editor-street preacher here provides the modern reader with insights into the Book of Genesis—with authority, humor, and awareness of the major influences on even the most sophisticated persons' mentality today.

—**$4.95,** Cloth

THEOLOGY AND SANITY by F. J. Sheed. This book has become a classic for its clear, concise analysis of the role of God in the lives of modern men and women.

—**$3.50,** Cloth

PASS IT ON by James Ewens, S.J. A guide for today's concerned parents for teaching the Faith to their children. With an appreciation of the author's success in helping mothers and fathers to understand the needs of their offspring by Dr. Christiane Brusselmans. Here is a straightforward presentation of the psychological and real-life influences parents must comprehend before assuming their rightful roles as the prime religious educators of their children.

—**$1.75,** Paper

THE EXPLOSION OF THE SUPERNATURAL by John Haffert. A review of recent spiritual phenomena, including the growing effect of the charismatic and pentecostal movements and the impact of religious manifestations on the spiritual lives of men and women of our times.

—**$1.95,** Paper

Cassette Tapes

ADAM AND EVE AND US. Frank Sheed, here recorded for the first time in studio conditions, gives his insightful views of the Book of Genesis in a style even the most sophisticated listener will appreciate. Tasteful humor and homely examples from contemporary developments enhance the presentation.

—**$29.95,** 4 cassetts (2 hours) with 12-page resource guide

IN SEARCH OF JESUS by F. J. Sheed. The author-publisher-street preacher here discusses, with a group of college students, the key subject of concern to millions in our times. Packaged in durable, attractive folder for convenient library storage.

—**$39.95,** 4 cassettes (4 hours)

HOW TO PRAY by Bernard Bassett, S.J. A world-famous preacher and retreat master perceptively guides American listeners to teach themselves to pray. Humorous but serious, the tapes provide a personal source for study, guidance, and inspiration.

—**$19.95,** 2 cassettes (2 hours)

ONE STEP ENOUGH FOR ME. Father Bernard Basset, S.J., draws on his twenty-five years of preaching retreats all over the world to help us to meet our daily anxieties and tensions. Packaged in durable, attractive folder for convenient library storage.

—**$19.95,** 2 cassettes (2 hours) with Discussion Guide

WHAT'S GOING ON IN THE CHURCH? Author-publisher Frank Sheed, adult education leader Mary Reed Newland, and theologian Dr. Anthony Padovano dialogue here on key questions of the times, directed by Father Arthur P. McNally, C.P., associate editor of *Sign* magazine. Each makes a statement which is then discussed by all. Key topics are: "Why Be a Catholic?", "Prayer," "What Christ Means to Me," and "The Church—Who's Minding It?"

—**$29.95,** 4 cassettes (4 hours)

Order Your Resource Materials Today From—

ARENA LETTRES
432 Park Avenue South, New York, N.Y. 10016

FRIENDS AREN'T KEPT WAITING
——copies, Paper, $1.75

ELIZABETH ANN SETON: Mother, Teacher,
Saint for Our Time
——copies, Paper, $1.50

THE GOSPEL OF THE HOLY SPIRIT
——copies, Paper, $1.50
——copies, Resource Guide, 75¢

GENESIS REGAINED
——copies, Cloth, $4.95

THEOLOGY AND SANITY
——copies, Cloth, $3.50

PASSING IT ON
——copies, Paper, $1.75

THE EXPLOSION OF THE SUPERNATURAL
——copies, Paper, $1.95

ADAM AND EVE AND US
——sets, $29.95

IN SEARCH OF JESUS
——sets, $39.95

HOW TO PRAY
——sets, $19.95

ONE STEP ENOUGH FOR ME
——sets, $19.95 including Discussion Guide

WHAT'S GOING ON IN THE CHURCH?
——sets, $29.95

NAME _____

ADDRESS _____

CITY _____ STATE _____ ZIP _____

——Payment enclosed (no shipping charge).
——Bill me (shipping extra).